NO LONGER THE
PROPERTY OF
ELON UNIVERSITY LIBRARY

D0239019

FIELD
EXPERIENCE

FIELD EXPERIENCE

METHODS OF REFLECTIVE TEACHING

SECOND EDITION

GEORGE J. POSNER
Cornell University

Longman
New York & London

953059

Field Experience: Methods of Reflective Teaching, Second Edition

Copyright © 1989 by Longman Inc. All rights reserved.
No part of this publication may be reproduced, stored
in a retrieval system, or transmitted in any form
or by any means, electronic, mechanical, photocopying,
recording, or otherwise, without the prior permission
of the publisher.

Longman Inc., 95 Church Street, White Plains, N. Y. 10601

Associated companies:
Longman Group Ltd., London
Longman Cheshire Pty., Melbourne
Longman Paul Pty., Auckland
Copp Clark Pitman, Toronto
Pitman Publishing Inc., New York

Executive editor: Raymond O'Connell
Production editor: Camilla T. K. Palmer
Text design: Jill Frances Wood
Cover design: Steven August Krastin
Director of production: Eduardo Castillo

Library of Congress Cataloging-in-Publication Data

Posner, George J.
  Field experience.

  Bibliography: p.
  Includes index.
  1. Student teaching. 2. Teaching—Vocational
guidance. 3. Teachers—Training of. I. Title.
LB2157.A3P6 1988   370'.7'33   88-9053
ISBN 0-8013-0291-9

94 93 92 91 90 89 9 8 7 6 5 4

To Prema and Becky

Contents

Preface

Field experience typically constitutes the centerpiece of any teacher education program. Early field experiences enable students to get their feet wet and to explore teaching as a profession. Later field experiences increase the students' responsibility for conducting classes and, more generally, help the students assume the full role of a teacher. Whether your field experience consists of tutoring a student in biology, working with a reading group, assisting an experienced English teacher with a whole class, or taking sole responsibility for teaching a social studies class, this book will help you to learn from the experience.

Since field experiences occur at various levels in teacher education programs, you could use this book as a guide from the beginning to the end of your program and into your first years of teaching. Generally speaking, the earlier you begin to use this book, the greater the benefit will be.

Three questions provide the focus of this book:

- How can you select an appropriate field experience in teaching?
- How can you prepare yourself for your field experience?
- How do your goals and perspectives on teaching change as a consequence of reflecting on your field experience?

Field Experience: Methods of Reflective Teaching is based on the premise that we benefit from our experiences by preparing for and reflecting on them. Preparation opens our eyes to the social and personal backgrounds of the people with whom we work. Reflection enables us to consider the consequences of our actions in light of our past experiences and the ideas derived from our formal study of education. Together, these two activities increase our ability to work in a thoughtful and appropriate manner rather than merely repeating mindlessly the practices of past teachers.

This book is intended to provoke thought; it is not a text filled with facts to memorize nor is it a handbook filled with dos and don'ts. If it is to stimulate reflection, you will have to do more than read this book. You will have to respond to questions, do exercises, analyze experiences, and state personal beliefs. In order to encourage this type of active involvement, the book provides space for you to write down your responses. Some of these devices will provoke more thought than others and, therefore, require more extensive and detailed responses. Some will help you work out problems you are having, while others will seem irrelevant to your particular field experience. For example, there is no point in trying to select an appropriate field experience if you have no choice in the matter. You should feel free to focus your attention on the questions and exercises that seem most pertinent to your situation.

Although the entire book is intended for use throughout a teacher education program, certain chapters are more appropriate for certain phases of the program than others. Chapters 1 to 3 are orientation chapters and are most useful before placement in a field experience. These three chapters help the selection of the most appropriate position. Chapters 4 to 10 are best used to help prepare for the field experience once the position is chosen. Chapter 11 helps direct reflection on the field experience as it nears completion. The Epilogue at the end of Chapter 11 assumes the completion of the field experience and suggests ways of reflecting on it and thereby preparing for the next field experience. The Appendix provides examples of actual student sample progress reports.

These chapters, therefore, present a cyclical approach to the field experiences in teacher education: preparation, engagement, and then reflection, thereby preparing for the next experience. This preparation-engagement-reflection-preparation cycle is aimed at making field experiences purposeful and reflective, thereby giving them a greater educational value.

The second edition represents a refinement of the basic text. More middle and high school examples and references correct the first edition's inadvertent overemphasis on elementary education. Chapters 7 and 10 have been somewhat streamlined in response to readers who found them too cumbersome. Several reviewers liked the Teacher Belief Inventory (TBI) in Chapter 8 so much that they recommended adding a pretest earlier in the book. Consequently, I have developed a Student Belief Inventory for Chapter 6, the responses to which can be compared with the TBI responses. Relations between reflective teaching and the psychological literature on metacognition have been added to Chapter 3. A section on observing a lesson using Madeline Hunter's basic lesson design has been added to Chapter 5. The subtitle has been slightly changed from "A Guide" to "Methods of." This change reflects my belief that this text is intended primarily as a resource of exercises and techniques for becoming more reflective as a teacher. As such, it is suitable for methods courses as well as early field experience courses and student teaching.

Acknowledgments

This book is in some ways a collage of ideas relevant to field experience in teaching. Although each chapter reveals the influence of many people and their writings, most chapters reflect the influence of one or two principal pieces of work.

The dominant influence on Chapter 1 was Joseph Schwab's notion of "commonplaces" in his 1971 *School Review* article, "The Practical: Translation into Curriculum." Chapter 2 has two sources: M. Cohen's Master's thesis at Ohio State University, "A Factor Analytic Study of Elementary School Student Teacher Concerns," as reported in Andrew Schwebel *et al., The Student Teacher Handbook* (Barnes and Noble, 1979), and Janet Sitter's dissertation from Michigan State University entitled, "The Student Teaching Experience from the Perspective of the Student Teacher." Chapter 3 is based on Carl Grant and Ken Zeichner's "On Becoming a Reflective Teacher" from the book edited by Carl Grant entitled, *Preparing for Reflective Teaching: A Book of Readings* (Allyn and Bacon, 1984). Chapters 4 and 5 derive from Dan Lortie's *School-teacher* (University of Chicago Press, 1975), Willard Waller's *The Sociology of Teaching* (John Wiley and Sons, 1932), and Rob A. Walker and Clem Adelman's *A Guide to Classroom Observation* (Methuen, 1975). The exercises in Chapter 6 were inspired by books like *Teaching Is* . . . by Merrill Harmin and Tom Gregory (SRA, 1974). Chapter 7 is based on many sources, including Tom Good and Jere Brophy's *Educational Psychology: A Realistic Approach,* 2nd ed. (Holt, Rinehart and Winston, 1977), and Michael Young's *Knowledge and Control* (Collier-Macmillan, 1971). However, the basic structure of the chapter and the issues addressed is based on Ann and Harold Berlak's *Dilemmas of Schooling* (Methuen, 1981). Chapter 8 draws on research carried out at the University of Wisconsin at Madison by Ken Zeichner and Bob Tabachnik (based on Berlak's work). Chapter 9 uses ideas from a 1982 *Science Education* article by Doug Roberts, "Developing the Concept of 'Curriculum Emphasis' in Science Education." Chapter 10 elaborates some ideas of Ed Smith and Neil Sendelbach presented in "The Programme, the Plans and the Activities of the Classroom: The Demands of Activity-based Science," a chapter in *Innovation in the Science Curriculum,* edited by John Olson (Nichols, 1982). Chapter 11 developed out of my own work with students at Cornell in a field-based course on teaching.

Beyond these specific contributions, the general orientation of the book derives from Ann and Harold Berlak's book, *Dilemmas in Schooling,* the many articles and papers on the student-teaching experience, and reflective teaching by Ken Zeichner and company (including Bob Tabachnick, Carl Grant, and Ken Teitelbaum) at the University of Wisconsin–Madison.

In addition to these major sources, criticisms of earlier drafts by Ken Zeichner and some of his students at Wisconsin, Richard Duschel at the University of Texas–Houston, Ken Strike at Cornell, Jeff Dean and his colleagues and students at SUC–Oneonta, and Al Rudnitsky and his students at Smith College, contributed greatly to the book.

My own students in Education 240, The Art of Teaching, not only criticized earlier drafts but also contributed numerous examples, logs, and progress reports incorporated into the present text. My secretary, Berni Oltz, battled the word processor and time constraints to transform mazelike drafts into the finished manuscript.

For all these contributions, I am deeply indebted, although any errors or omissions are, of course, my responsibility.

PART 1
Orientation

CHAPTER 1

What Do Field Experiences Have in Common?

The one indispensable part of any teacher preparation program is field experience. Student teaching can be considered a special type of field experience. It is so special that it is given a specific name and preferred status within preservice programs. In certain respects, however, all field experiences are similar. In this chapter we will discuss some common features of all preservice field experiences. These common features will serve us in subsequent chapters as a map on which to locate the concerns, goals, and issues faced by all students about to begin preservice field experiences.

COMMON FEATURES

All teaching situations have four features in common.[1] Although these four features may seem too obvious to mention or simply appear to reflect common sense, they will be useful reference points. First, almost by definition a teaching situation must include a *teacher* or teachers of some sort. (The term *teaching agent* could be used to include texts or machines that teach, such as programmed instruction.) Second, there is at least one *learner* (termed *pupil* or *student*, depending upon how old or how serious about learning the person is). Third, there is some *subject matter* or material that the teacher shares with, presents to, or negotiates with the learner; that is, there is something that the teacher teaches (the "stuff" of teaching), be it academic knowledge, personal feelings, or technical skills.

There is always a danger that a teaching situation will lack the necessary balance of these three features. When teaching ignores the learner, there is a tendency to be autocratic; when it ignores the teacher, it tends to be laissez-faire; when it ignores the subject matter, it is typically empty.

This "triad"[2] occurs within the fourth feature of a teaching situation— a social and physical *context* consisting of rules, facilities, values, expectations, and personal backgrounds, which act as resources, constraints, and direct influences on teaching and learning. Figure 1.1 summarizes these features.

When we think of teachers, learners, subject matter, and context, many issues come to mind. Each of these features serves as a category of issues for a discussion about educational topics. In fact, if these four features are truly comprehensive, we would expect all educational issues to fall into one or more of these categories.

Teachers

When we consider the teacher, we are addressing issues such as the following:

- The kind of person the teacher should be
- The proper role of the teacher
- The reasons people chose teaching as a career and stay in or leave the profession

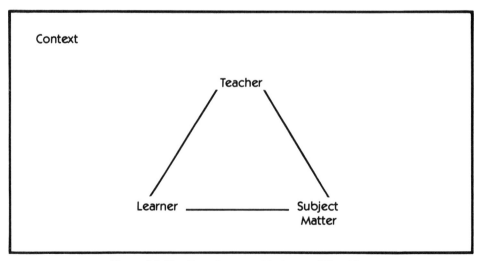

Figure 1.1 The Four Common Features of Teaching

- The reasons teachers burn out or remain fresh
- The tasks teachers face in classrooms

Learners

In a sense, we are and will always be learners, regardless of our age or position. Obviously the range of potential learners is immense, particularly if we consider not only ages but also purposes, aspirations, and backgrounds. We must also consider that this diversity greatly affects any teaching. Furthermore, there is quite a difference between teaching in a 1:1 situation and teaching a large group of diverse individuals. In 1:1 (or one-to-*small* group) situations issues such as the following arise regarding the learner:

- What the learner already knows
- What comes easily or with difficulty
- What learners consider to be relevant
- The anxieties that must be taken into account
- The learner's future career
- What the learner is likely to find interesting, stimulating, or challenging

When teaching a group of learners, additional issues arise:

- The treatment of learners, as unique individuals or as members of categories (e.g., gifted and talented, non-college bound)
- The degree to which learners should be treated equally or differently
- Whether the fastest, the middle, or the slowest learners should be used as a reference for decisions about when to move on to new material (i.e., pacing)
- Whether the teacher should try to develop a sense of "groupness"

Subject Matter

What teachers teach ranges from facts and concepts to thinking processes, to physical skills, to values and feelings. One issue of concern is the relative importance of each of these domains of subject matter. For example, we might question the legitimacy of using the teacher's or the learner's own feelings as subject matter for instruction. Or we might try to decide whether to regard subject matter as truths to be learned or to emphasize how truth is reached.

Another important issue concerns the fact that time is a very scarce commodity. We simply do not have the time to teach everything as completely as we would desire. Therefore, we always seem to be faced with the "breadth versus depth" issue. For example, how much should we try to cover and to what extent should we take the time to get all the students to understand the material fully? How do we reconcile these often conflicting demands for coverage and mastery?

Context

Students and classrooms are unique places that do not change very much. They have distinctive physical and social qualities that persist from generation to generation. Philip Jackson[3] asks us to imagine entering a school at night with nobody else there and all the lights off. The smell alone would tell us where we are. The distinctive smells of cleaning fluids, chalk dust, and pencil shavings would give it away. Turning on the lights would confirm our location.

> School bulletin boards may be changed but they are never discarded, the seats may be arranged but thirty of them are there to stay, the teacher's desk may have a new plant on it but there it sits, as ubiquitous as the roll-down maps, the olive drab wastebaskets, and the pencil sharpener on the window ledge.[4]

In terms of social context the classroom is also highly unique and stable. The makeup of classes and the faculty does not change drastically during the year. The conditions are almost always crowded. "Only in schools do thirty or more people spend several hours each day literally side by side. Once we leave the classroom we seldom are required to have contact with so many people for so long a time."[5] The daily schedule, types of classroom activity (e.g., seatwork, teacher demonstration), and rules (e.g., "keep your eyes on your own paper during tests") are highly uniform.

> Life there [in school] resembles life in other contexts in some ways, but not all. There is, in other words, a uniqueness to the student's world. School, like church and home, is someplace special. Look where you may, you will not find another place quite like it.[6]

Context includes all that contrains, facilitates, or otherwise influences what teachers and learners do with subject matter. Context, therefore, includes the immediate physical and social environment of the classroom. But it also includes the administration of the school, parental influences, the media (especially television), laws, court decisions, governmental regulations, the backgrounds of learners and teachers, the money available to finance education, and the time available for teaching.

From a broader viewpoint, the school is one of society's most pervasive institutions and, as such, can be held responsible for any contribution it may have made to societal problems. Even if the school is not responsible for these problems, some people see it as a powerful force for reforming society.

Institutions and agencies other than schools also offer distinctive contexts that influence teaching. For example, the 4-H program, the Boy Scouts and Girl Scouts, and other youth groups may not have buildings and rooms built solely for their meetings, but their meeting places still affect them. Furthermore, youth groups operate within distinctive social contexts, often highlighted by rituals (or pledges and oaths). Some groups specify special clothing (uniforms), badges, and handbooks or manuals. Each of these aspects of the social and physical environment influences any teaching that takes place in the youth groups.

Issues derived from the contextual aspects of teaching include the following:

- The amount of input that parents should have into the program of the school or group
- The extent to which the problems facing teachers and learners are due to problems in the society at large, in the organization of schools, in the individual learner, or in the learner's family
- The extent to which the teacher or group leader can or should criticize the policies and practices of the government, the schools, the youth group or agency, or other teachers or co-workers, and the extent to which the teacher or group leaders should try to encourage such criticism by the learner
- The value of using the community at large as an educational resource

The Four Common Features as a Whole

It would be difficult, if not impossible, to think of teaching with any of these four features missing. Teaching without someone or something doing the teaching sounds absurd. Teaching without someone to teach sounds like a charade. Teaching without something to teach sounds like a waste of everybody's time. Teaching without any context sounds impossible.

Not only are all features necessary, they are also of equal importance. These four features comprise the whole of the phenomenon that we call education.[7] Any particular conception of education, whether psychological, sociological, or philosophical, provides at best one perspective of this whole, and, more typically, one perspective on one facet of the whole. Care must be exercised if we are to maintain an approach that includes the whole of teaching. Concern with maintaining our role as teachers should not blind us to the ways in which the learner learns best. Concern for covering the subject matter should not blind us to the needs of the learners. Concern for the learner's feelings should not obscure the community's expectations and the value of learning the subject matter. Neither the learner, nor the subject matter, nor the physical and social content, nor our own needs as teachers should be allowed to dominate. All four features must be coordinated so that balance is achieved.

The set of four features provides a map on which to locate each concern relative to the others. The set not only suggests that from each perspective we will "see *some* part of the whole . . . [but also] enables [us] to know—to some degree, at any rate—*what* part of the whole [we] will see."[8]

The common features of teaching have been expressed in somewhat abstract terms in order to make them an all-purpose way of discussing any teaching situation. Now we will try to make them more concrete.

VARIETIES OF TEACHING SITUATIONS

No two field experiences are identical. One way to describe their differences is to refer to the four common features. We shall begin by examining the range of experiences you have already had (using the four common features) and conclude by identifying the types of experiences you are lacking.

When one of my classes was about to embark on an exploratory field experience, I asked them to make an inventory of their previous teaching experience. They responded with a very wide range of teaching situations.

1. Teaching first aid to kindergarten classes
2. Teaching balloon sculpturing to college classmates
3. Teaching long-duration hiking to a 4-H group
4. Teaching piano to a sister
5. Being a counselor at the county jail
6. Tutoring history to a tenth grader
7. Teaching a little brother to bowl
8. Teaching horseback riding to kids ages 4–15 at summer camp
9. Teaching a younger brother how to tie his shoes
10. Coaching the debating team
11. Teaching new routines and correcting moves as sergeant in color guard
12. Teaching a friend how to change a car's oil
13. Teaching a sister the evils of cigarette smoking (or trying to)
14. Teaching a driver-education class on drunken driving
15. Teaching backgammon to mother
16. Teaching Morse code in the Navy
17. Teaching a friend to meditate

EXERCISE 1.1   Inventory of Teaching Experiences

You probably have had more experience as a teacher than you realize. Maybe you took charge of a group such as scouts, 4-H, summer camp, or a club in high school. If you were responsible for what the group learned from the experience, you were a teacher. Maybe you tried to tutor someone. You might have been an official tutor. Or perhaps your friend, brother, or sister needed something explained or demonstrated. Even as a baby-sitter you might have had to explain or demonstrate something occasionally. The subject matter might have ranged from algebra to sharing toys to tying shoes. This exercise is intended to help inventory past experience as a teacher. Completing it should result in a greater awareness of previous teaching experience and a more informal basis for choosing future field experiences. Use Form 1.1 to list your teaching experiences.

FORM 1.1. INVENTORY OF TEACHING EXPERIENCES

Experience	Subject matter	Learner's age or grade level	Context (e.g., school, camp, youth group)	Ways different from you (e.g., racial, cultural, socioeconomic)
0	Swimming	Age 7–9	Summer camp	City kids
1				
2				
3				
4				
5				

The experiences spanned a wide range of learners, subject matter, and contexts. The learners ranged from 4-year-old children to a 40-year-old mother. The subject matter ranged from physical skills (such as shoe tying, bowling, piano playing, and changing a car's oil), to factual knowledge (such as history and Morse code), to attitudes and values (such as emotional problems of prisoners and the evils of cigarette smoking), to intellectual skills (such as debating). The contexts ranged from one-to-one tutoring and counseling to one-to-30 teaching, and from educational institutions, such as schools and colleges, to youth groups and service agencies (4-H, Big Brothers, etc.), to families and friendships, and even to the armed forces.

It might be useful to examine each of your prior teaching experiences in terms of the learners, the subject matter, and the context in order to determine their range. Also consider your range of teaching experiences with people different from yourself. Use the space provided in Form 1.1 to identify these features of your experiences. How wide a range of experiences have you had? What types of experiences are you lacking? Are any of these worth pursuing at this time?

▶

You should now have gained a broader perspective on field experiences, both those you have had and those that are still in front of you.

1. With what sorts of learners might you work? How old? What type of family background? Any special physical, emotional, or intellectual characteristics?

▶

2. What subject matter might you teach? Physical skills, attitudes, values, feelings? Facts and concepts? Intellectual skills? A mixture of these or some other type of subject matter? Might you teach "academic" subject matter or "life skills" needed to get along after schooling?

▶

3. In what context might the teaching take place? Individual or group? In what institution? Schools? Curricular or extracurricular? What levels? Social agencies? Youth groups? Any special characteristics of the context?

▶

4. With what sorts of teachers might you work?

▶

THE STUDENT-TEACHING EXPERIENCE

Seen within this framework of teachers, learners, subject matter, and context, student teaching is a very special type of field experience.

The reader will notice these arrows used throughout the text. They indicate that a reader response is expected.

Learners

The learners may come from a wide range of socioeconomic and ethnic backgrounds, some of which may be quite foreign to the student teacher. The learners may also represent a broad spectrum of abilities and may range from those bordering on the mentally retarded to those considered to be geniuses. To some extent, every student-teaching experience is unique, since every learner is unique.

Subject Matter

With the extent of their background in some school subject matter, some student teachers take that subject matter for granted, believing that others consider it important, straightforward, interesting, and not too difficult to learn. It is important to remember, however, that most of the subject matter taught in schools is taught nowhere else and is, therefore, somewhat esoteric. In addition, English, social studies, science, math, art, or physical education may be easy and fun for the person who has majored in the subject but may be difficult or boring for many others. Furthermore, the learners' parents may have learned something very different in the subject when they attended school. Finally, the student teacher may conceive of the subject matter in terms of just facts and concepts, but he or she is also teaching values and attitudes, if not explicitly then at least by example and by use of stated and unstated classroom rules. (See Chapter 7 for a more extended discussion of the "hidden curriculum.")

Context

Of the four features, the social context and, in particular, the role of the student teacher distinguish student teaching most from all other teaching situations. The student teacher can be considered a junior partner to the cooperating teacher.[9] This role restricts both the student teacher's classroom responsibilities and opportunities for experimentation. The student teacher is not typically seen as an equal member of a teaching team, a role some professional teachers achieve; nor is the student teacher autonomous, a role most professional teachers prefer; nor is the student teacher merely an aide, since cooperating teachers typically expect the student teachers to assume increased responsibility during the term. To complicate matters further, the student teacher answers not only to the cooperating teacher but also to the college supervisor. The student teacher is still a college student and, typically, the college supervisor assigns a grade based on the supervisor's observations and the cooperating teacher's recommendations. It is unlikely that the student teacher will ever again be in a situation quite like this one. It is at the same time exciting, frustrating, and ultimately fulfilling.

NOTES

1. See Joseph Schwab, "The Practical: Arts of Eclectic," *School Review* 79 (1971), 493–542. He terms my four common features "commonplaces."
2. David Hawkins, "I, Thou, It," *Mathematics Teaching*, Journal of the British Association of Teachers of Mathematics, No. 46, Spring 1969.
3. Philip Jackson, *Life in Classrooms* (New York: Holt, Rinehart and Winston, 1968).
4. Ibid., pp. 6–7.
5. Ibid., p. 8.
6. Ibid., p. 9.
7. See Schwab, op. cit., for the source of this discussion.
8. Schwab, op. cit., p. 339 (italics in original).
9. Janet Sitter and Perry Lanier, "Student Teaching: A Stage in the Development of a Teacher? Or a Period of Consolidation?" Paper presented at the Annual Meeting of the American Educational Research Association, New York, March 1982.

CHAPTER 2

What Are Your Concerns and Personal Goals Regarding Field Experiences?

This chapter is intended to aid in the planning of your upcoming field experience. It will help you to make explicit the concerns that you have as you anticipate this experience and to discover the feelings of other people in similar situations. Finally, this chapter will help you to identify personal goals that you might want to achieve during your field experience.

EXERCISE 2.1 Expressing Concerns

Take a moment to express your primary concerns regarding your field experience. What worries you or occupies your mind about it? For example, in what ways do you feel that you will not measure up? That the experience will not be what you really want? In what ways do you feel that you will be disappointed? What really counts for your satisfaction with the experience? Make a list of these concerns in the space below:

▶ 1.

2.

3.

4.

5.

6.

ANALYZING CONCERNS

Now we will analyze expressed concerns by using the four features of teaching (from Chapter 1) as categories of analysis. Doing this will help to stimulate further thinking about concerns.

Learners

Who the learners are, what they are like, and how to respond to them as individuals are likely to be one area of concern. Consider the following concerns, taken from a study by Cohen and associates (1972) as reported by Schwebel *et al.* (1979).[1] The numbers in parentheses give the percentage of the 139 elementary school student teachers surveyed who reported these concerns as causing them moderate to very great concern.

1. Discovering and developing the potential talents of each child (76.3)
2. Presenting the work in ways that engage the students' interest (74.0)
3. Adapting assignments to the needs of the individual student (69.8)
4. Working with students who don't seem to care if they learn or not (81.3)

Subject Matter

Teaching subject matter effectively is usually an area of concern expressed in terms of covering the material and helping learners really to understand and apply it. For example:

1. Teaching students to think through problems on their own (71.2)
2. Finding sufficient time to cover the required material effectively (61.2)
3. Getting students to apply what they have learned to new problems (63.3)
4. Presenting material in ways that foster understanding (64.0)

Context

Concern for effectively managing groups of learners involves establishing and enforcing rules, creating a climate conducive to learning, maintaining it, and restoring it constructively when necessary.[2] Such a climate is necessary to minimize the disruptive effects that one individual can have on the group and to maximize the educational benefits to all members of the group. For example:

1. Finding ways to control the students effectively (72.6)
2. Dealing with students who interfere with others' work (70.4)
3. Providing all the pupils with opportunities for class participation (55.4)
4. Dealing with classroom troublemakers (68.4)

Although these concerns are expressed in classroom terms, they apply to work within any group context (e.g., Boy Scouts). In one-to-one teaching situations such as tutoring, concerns might include:

1. Maintaining support from the teacher and the family
2. Finding a place to work with minimal distractions
3. Finding the necessary resources

Teachers

Concern with being a competent professional typically involves being knowledgeable, being perceived as competent, and continually improving one's methods. For example:

1. Not falling into routine methods of presenting material (69.1)
2. Finding ways of keeping up with new ideas in education (57.5)
3. Achieving a good understanding of personal strengths and weaknesses with respect to teaching (56.8)

Do your expressed concerns refer primarily to the learners, the subject matter, the context, or yourself as a professional teacher? How similar are your concerns to those of other people beginning a preservice field experience?
▶

The concerns that you have about your upcoming field experience will greatly affect the ways in which you will benefit from it. Serious concerns can become anxieties and uncertainties that can lead to nervousness or even depression. Nobody wants that. Instead, the analysis of concerns is intended to increase the benefit of the field experience. In order for you to benefit from an examination of concerns, however, you must translate the concerns into actions. In order to do this, you have to formulate goals and plans based on your concerns.

EXERCISE 2.2   Expressing Personal Goals and Priorities

People's goals affect their actions, expectations, and perceptions, even (and maybe especially) when the people are unaware of these goals. Expressing goals makes their examination possible, thereby providing an opportunity for reassessment.

Write a few sentences describing how you expect to benefit from your field experience.

▶

Now look at what you have written. You might want to compare your goals with the following ones:

1. To find out what teaching is really like (i.e., career exploration)
2. To see if I like teaching (i.e., exploring personal preferences)
3. To see if I can really do it (i.e., self-testing)
4. To learn some skills and modify certain habits and characteristics (i.e., training)
5. To develop my own approach or style (i.e., personal style)
6. To apply what I've learned in college to real students and to real classrooms (i.e., theory into practice)

Try considering each of your goals as a variation of one of the six general goal types listed above. If this matching does no violence to your goals, label your goals 1–6, according to which general goal type each represents. Try to rank order your own goals or the six goal types above according to how important each is to you for this particular field experience.

▶ 1.
   2.
   3.
   4.
   5.
   6.

What do you conclude? Do you view your field experience primarily as exploratory (goals 1 and 2), as a time to test yourself (goal 3), as a training period (goal 4), as a search for personal identity (goal 5), or as an extension of your college education (goal 6)? Where are your current priorities?

▶

Goals may be experienced sequentially. Early field experiences might be exploratory (goals 1 and 2) and offer an opportunity to get your feet wet, to examine teaching from the other side of the desk. The next set of field experiences might provide a chance to learn some techniques of teaching (goal 4 and perhaps 5). These intermediate field experiences can serve as a time to learn everything possible about teaching. Courses late in the teacher education program might provide a knowledge base on which to teach (goal 6). Janet Sitter[3] found just such a progression in the "interns" she supervised. She found, however, that as they began to prepare for student teaching, their goals changed. "She no longer expressed a desire to learn all there is to know. . . . Now [that] she had been taught to teach, it was her task to go into the classroom and prove that she had learned; that she could do it."[4] That is, the students began to view student teaching less as "practice teaching" (goal 4), and more as a "proving ground" (goal 3). I mention this progression from goal 4 to goal 3 not as something student teachers should strive for, but only as an example of the way people shift goals during their teacher preparation program. Goals are tentative, not permanent.

For some students, developing a personal style or approach (goal 5) might be relevant at every level of their program. For others, it might not be seriously considered until their second or third year of regular employment, after they have survived the often traumatic first year of professional teaching. However, regardless of the pressure and intensity of the experience, goal 5 is certainly compatible with all the others and is a worthwhile ongoing goal for every field experience.

EXERCISE 2.3 Setting Specific Goals

Once you have formulated personal goals to guide your field experience, it might be productive to set more specific goals. In order to do this, consider again each of the general goal types.

Goal 1: To find out what teaching is really like

Are there some specific kinds of teaching situations you would like to explore? (Refer back to your responses on page 9 in Chapter 1.)

Learners. Are there some specific kinds of learners about whom you want to learn? Ones with special problems? Gifted or talented ones? Particular ages? Particular ethnic backgrounds?

▶

Subject matter. Is there some particular subject matter you want to try teaching? A particular school subject? A sport? Do you have some specialty you want to try?

▶

Context. Are there any contexts that you want to explore? Particular youth groups or social agencies? Particular size groups? Team teaching? Open classrooms? Communities with special characteristics?

▶

Teacher. Would you like to work with or under a particular type of teacher? One with a certain philosophy or approach? One with a special type of training or background? A particular ethnic background?

▶

Goal 2: To see if you really like teaching

Are there some specific types of teaching activities that you want to try? These might include leading a discussion, giving a lecture, setting up a role play, one-to-one tutoring, helping a child with personal problems, discussing a controversial issue with a class, dealing with a disruptive child, assigning grades, meeting with a parent, designing and teaching a unit or a lesson, setting up and then teaching a laboratory lesson, doing a demonstration.

▶

Goal 3: To see if you can really do it

To whom do you want to prove yourself? To yourself? To a group of learners? To your college supervisor? To parents? To the cooperating teacher? To aides? Do you want to "lead" and be recognized as "the leader"? Be recognized by whom?

▶

For many teachers in training, when others recognize their leadership, they report "feeling like a teacher."[5] Developing a teacher identity plays an important role in proving oneself.[6]

Goal 4: To learn some skills and modify certain habits and characteristics

What particular skills do you want to learn? What instructional techniques?

▶

Your goals may derive from what you regard as the keys to successful teaching. For example, most student teachers attribute successful teaching either to general good planning or to well-executed lessons, although some also specify "challenging" or "interesting" lessons, ones they enjoy themselves, giving clear directions and providing variety (change of pace).[7] Developing these sorts of teaching skills might be important to you. In addition to instructional techniques, organization and management techniques might have a high priority. For Sitter's[8] student teachers, this meant:

> *successfully getting a group of learners through a lesson or series of lessons within a limited amount of time. It meant creating a classroom climate conducive to learning; maintaining this environment and restoring the climate constructively when necessary.[9]*

In addition to skills, are there certain habits, traits, or characteristics that you want to acquire or modify? Do you believe, as did some of Sitter's[10] student teachers, that your ability to teach will be hindered by a "lack of patience, low tolerance level, shyness, inadequate feelings, insecurities,"[11] "poor time assessment, lack of creativity, general lack of knowledge in either the scope or sequence of content,"[12] "lack of ambition, hyperactivity, aggressiveness, or lack of commitment"?[13] Obviously, attempts to change such personal propensities are at best frustrating and at worst impossible. But identifying them and explicitly working on them in a field experience might at least allow you to accept them and then to compensate for them.
▶

Goal 5. To develop your own approach or style

What makes you unique as a teacher? What do you stand for and believe in?
▶

This goal is actually something that you will achieve as you work through this book. Your own personal perspective on teaching is, in one sense, your own approach. What approaches to, or styles of, teaching would you like to learn about in the process of developing your own? Can you find anyone who epitomizes your ideal teacher?
▶

Goal 6. To apply what you have learned in college to real learners and to real classrooms

Are there any specific concepts or theories you want to apply—for example, theories of group dynamics, developmental theories, personality theories, learning theories, motivational theories, or sociological theories? What will you look for in your field experience in order to make the application?
▶

Having considered all these goals, try to specify your personal goals, and list them in order of priority.

▶

What follows is an example of the goals mentioned by one prospective elementary school student teacher:

- To learn more about implementing a language-experience approach to reading
- To work on some sort of "discipline teachnique"—learning to feel out where you have to draw the line and how far it can go before you have to start saying "all right, sit down," etc.
- To become more sensitive to the feelings and needs of individual children ("getting to know the children faster")
- To develop more confidence as a teacher—specifically, wanted to develop the ability to "change course" in the middle of a lesson when the children were not responding to what was planned

With your goals in mind, write down what plans you will make in order to reach your goals or at least to move in that direction.

▶

NOTES

1. Andrew Schwebel *et al.*, *The Student Teacher Handbook* (New York: Barnes and Noble,1979).
2. Janet Sitter, "The Student Teaching Experience from the Perspective of the Student Teacher: A Descriptive Study." Unpublished doctoral dissertation, Michigan State University, 1982.
3. Ibid.
4. Ibid., p. 127.
5. Ibid.
6. Ibid.
7. Ibid., pp. 136–139.
8. Ibid.
9. Ibid., p. 139.
10. Ibid.
11. Ibid., p. 148.
12. Ibid., p. 149.
13. Ibid., p. 149.

CHAPTER 3

Why and How Should You Reflect on Your Field Experience?

Experience + Reflection = Growth

As this equation suggests (and as John Dewey has argued), we do not actually learn from experience as much as we learn from reflecting on experience.

This chapter will help you to document and begin to reflect on your field experience. There are many possible ways to become more reflective about teaching. This book uses two methods, in-text questions/exercises and logs or journals. Before these methods are explained, however, an explanation of reflective thinking is necessary.

WHAT IS REFLECTIVE THINKING AND WHY IS IT DESIRABLE?

Reflective thinking means "turning a subject over in the mind and giving it serious and consecutive consideration."[1] Dewey insists that reflective thinking frees us from mere "impulsive" and "routine activity."[2] "It enables us to act in deliberate and intentional fashion" to achieve what we need. It distinguishes us as human beings and is the hallmark of intelligent (as opposed to mere "appetitive, blind and impulsive") action.[3]

Nonreflective teachers rely on routine behavior and are guided more by impulse, tradition, and authority than by reflection. They simplify their professional lives by uncritically accepting everyday reality in schools. They can then "concentrate their efforts on finding the most effective and efficient means to achieve ends and to solve problems that have largely been defined for them by others."[4] In contrast, reflective teachers actively, persistently, and carefully consider and reconsider beliefs and practices "in light of the grounds that support them and the further consequences to which they lead."[5]

Reflective thinking allows the teacher to examine critically the assumptions that schools make about what can count as acceptable goals and methods, problems and solutions. Although we all must live within some constraints, often we accept as predetermined by authority or tradition far more than is necessary.

In your field experience, reflective thinking will allow you to act in deliberate and intentional ways, to devise new ways of teaching rather than being a slave to tradition, and to interpret new experiences from a fresh perspective.

As the equation that begins this chapter suggests, reflection with no experience is sterile and generally leads to unworkable conclusions. Experience with no reflection is shallow and at best leads to superficial knowledge. If you merely "do" your field experience without thinking deeply about it, if you merely allow your experiences to wash over you without savoring and examining them for their significance, your growth will be greatly limited. The logs you write, the questions you try to answer, and other activities in which you engage are all merely tools to facilitate reflective thinking about your field experience.

Is It Possible for an Effective Teacher to Reflect?

As necessary as reflective teaching may seem to some people, others are unconvinced. They argue that there is no *time* for reflection if at the same time you must teach effectively, that there is no *point* to reflection if you always have to do what you are told anyway, and that reflection is not *necessary*, because you can be a good teacher without it. Let us examine these three objections one at a time.[6]

Is There Time. Philip Jackson[7] reminds us that classrooms are busy places:

> [An elementary] teacher engages in as many as 1000 interpersonal interchanges each day. . . . Teaching commonly involves talking and the teacher acts as a gatekeeper who manages the flow of the classroom dialogue. . . . Another time-consuming task for the teacher . . . is that of serving as supply sergeant. Classroom space and material resources

are limited and the teacher must allocate these resources judiciously. . . .
Broken pens and parched throats obviously do not develop one at a time
in an orderly fashion. . . . Closely related to the job of doling out material resources is that of granting special privileges to deserving students.
In elementary classrooms it is usually the teacher who assigns coveted
duties, such as serving on the safety patrol, or running the movie projec-
tor, or clapping the erasers. . . . A fourth responsibility of the teacher is
that of serving as an official timekeeper. In many schools he is assisted
in this job by elaborate systems of bells and buzzers. But even when the
school day is mechanically punctuated by clangs and hums, the teacher is
not entirely relieved of his responsibility.[8]

Jackson further points out that this "beehive of activity" is necessi-
tated by the "crowded condition" of the classroom. It is the "press of numbers and of time that keeps the teacher so busy."[9]

As of the realities of classrooms were not enough, institutional constraints further limit the teacher's time for reflection. Teachers are rarely
granted released time for reflection. There is continual pressure to cover a
specified curriculum and to ensure that a highly diverse group of children—
who attend school by compulsion rather than voluntarily—attain at least a
minimal level of achievement.

Jackson (among others) argues that, given these conditions, there is no
time for reflection and that reflection, if attempted, could only lead to pa-
ralysis of action and therefore less effective response to immediate circumstances.[10]

The immediacy of classroom life, the fleeting and sometimes cryptic signs
on which the teacher relies for determining his pedagogical moves and for
evaluating the effectiveness of his actions calls into question the appropriateness of using conventional models of rationality to depict the teacher's
classroom behavior when a teacher is standing before his students. . . .
The spontaneity, immediacy and irrationality of the teacher's behavior
seems to be its most salient characteristics. At such times there appears
to be a high degree of uncertainty, unpredictability, and even confusion
about the events in the classroom.[11]

But Jackson is also careful to point out another aspect of teaching:

The fact that the teacher does not appear to be very analytic or delibera-
tive in his moment-to-moment dealings with students should not obscure
the fact that there *are* times when this is not true. During periods of soli-
tude, in particular, before and after his face-to-face encounter with students, the teacher often seems to be engaged in a type of intellectual activ-

ity that has many of the formal properties of a problem-solving procedure. At such moments the teacher's work does look highly rational.

This brief mention of the teacher's behavior during moments when he is not actively engaged with students calls attention to an important division in the total set of teaching responsibilities. There is a crucial difference it would seem between what the teacher does when he is alone at his desk and what he does when his room fills up with students.[12]

Research is increasingly confirming the belief that the quality of teacher planning outside the classroom (what Jackson terms the "preactive" phase of teaching) influences the quality of teaching within the classroom (what Jackson terms the "interactive" phase).

Furthermore, despite the time constraints of classroom life, a certain degree of reflection is still possible in the "interactive" phase of teaching. There are always lulls in the action and even the fast pace of teaching requires some self-evaluation. To consider only the extremes of too much thought and blind action is to limit our options. Clearly, there needs to be a balance between thought and action.

What's the Point? Some people argue that there is little point in reflecting on goals and practices, when all the teacher does is implement someone else's ideas. They contend that "teachers are basically functionaries within a bureaucratic system; they have prescribed roles and responsibilities and in order to survive in that system they must always give way to institutional demands."[13] Furthermore, (some claim) teachers inevitably conform to the norms of the school, which "washes out" any reflectiveness left over from preservice training.[14]

Although it is true that schools do socialize new teachers into a dominant "teacher culture," there are a wide range of viewpoints represented in that culture.[15] Teachers within the same school vary widely in evaluation and classroom-management practices, goals, political beliefs, treatment of special pupils, adherence to textbooks, and friendliness versus businesslike roles. Surely there is ample room for teachers to exercise individuality in teaching while working within the constraints of schools.

As with our discussion of time, there are two extremes on this issue. According to one view, every teacher is an individual, a person who is free to implement an educational philosophy by teaching what and how he or she wishes. Counter to this sociologically naive view is the position that the forces of bureaucratic socialization in schools are strong and efficient.[16] As with most extreme views, there exists a more moderate position. This view asserts the "constant interplay between choice and constraint" in teaching.[17] Teachers, as professionals working within a powerful institution, have the opportunity to shape their identity, to take a stand even when they are in conflict with others, and to question common practices. Yes, teachers do implement someone else's ideas, but there is always room for personal judgment, decision, and criticism.

Recent psychological research supports this view. In contrast to both a behavioristic view (see B. F. Skinner's *Beyond Freedom and Dignity*) that a person's behavior is totally shaped by the environment, and a humanistic view (see Carl Rogers's *Freedom to Learn in the 1980s*) that a person is free to respond as he or she chooses, a cognitive view stresses the interplay between the individual and the environment. In particular, this view suggests that the individual monitors his or her own actions and thought processes and actively makes decisions about what, and even how, to think.

This latter aspect of mental activity psychologists term *metacognition*, which simply means thinking about thinking. Metacognition in teaching includes the ability of teachers to examine their own concepts, theories, and beliefs about teaching, learning, and their subject-matter, and the ability to monitor their decisions about what and how they teach. In a sense, metacognition is a psychological approach to reflective teaching.

Is It Really Necessary? Many claim that reflection is not necessary for teaching. Intuition, they argue, is more important for effective teaching than careful analytic thought. In fact some of the very best teachers do not seem to spend time reflecting on their work.

Much of this argument, and my response to it, follows the earlier discussion of time available for reflection. But there is more. Anybody who has tried to persuade a group of teachers to implement a particular curriculum has remarked at the degree to which teachers *adapt* rather than *adopt* curricula. Some curriculum developers have even gone to the extreme of attempting (in vain) to produce so-called teacher-proof curricula, an effort which I view as an affront to the profession of teaching. That such attempts have been generally unsuccessful seems to be sufficient evidence that teachers are very selective about what they will incorporate into their classrooms. Teachers work within a practicality ethic that subjects any innovation to a test of cost versus benefit, feasibility, and consistency within the teachers' perceptions of themselves and their situations.[18] It is no wonder, then, that most innovations are "blunted on the classroom door."[19] The view of teachers that emerges from studies of curriculum implementation is one of active professionals constantly making educational decisions for their particular classrooms.

Once again the two extremes are unworkable. Teachers operate neither on pure intuition nor on pure rational analysis. Teachers neither blindly adopt the materials and methods developed by "experts," nor insist on reinventing the wheel. Instead, teachers (especially effective ones) balance intuitive and reflective thought, using any resources they can find and adapting materials to suit their own purposes and methods.

How to Become More Reflective

As was mentioned earlier, there are two principle means used to help you reflect on your field experience: in-text questions/exercises and logs. Throughout the text are questions and exercises designed to encourage reflective thought. If you take these questions and exercises seriously, you will find yourself engaged in an inquiry about teaching that ultimately requires a degree of self-analysis and appraisal. The questions and exercises will lead you to develop a sense of approach to your teaching, a "perspective" that will help you define your professional identity. If you pursue a career in teaching, and you continue to reflect on your professional experience, your perspective will change over the years. These changes will constitute an important aspect of professional growth.

But there is a danger in making vague generalizations about teaching, because different situations require different perspectives. You need a way to focus a perspective on specific field experiences rather than on teaching in general. Your logs will help you use your field experience as a specific reference point for your perspective. When you finish this field experience, you probably will not have developed a comprehensive framework for all of education, but you likely will have determined where you stand and what you believe in with regard to your specific situation. This will be no small accomplishment!

Daily or weekly logs, journals, or some such method for recording events and personal reactions is one widely used device. Although somewhat time-consuming, written records and analyses provide a unique opportunity to keep track of events and privately to reflect on the personal and public meaning of those events. What happened? Why did it happen? What was my role? What beliefs did my actions reflect? Did my actions reflect beliefs and assumptions about which I was not aware? Did the consequences of my actions raise doubts or reinforce my beliefs? How should I want to act in the future on the basis of what happened?

The person that supervises your field experience may stipulate a preferred or required format for your log or journal. If this is the case, obviously you should follow it. However, if you have a relatively free hand in terms of format, this chapter will suggest one approach.

WHAT IS THE ANATOMY OF A LOG?

Because a lesson seems unproblematic, even uneventful, it does not mean that there is nothing to observe. The essence of observation is the creation of insight out of what might seem initially to be routine and commonplace. Hidden beneath the surface of this lesson are unresolved issues which, when they are made visible, reveal possible alternative beliefs, values and practice.[20]

Whether we call it a log or a journal does not matter. What does matter is to have an opportunity to think about field experiences. It is difficult to think deeply about all our experiences. Therefore, I suggest a format that helps to focus thoughts on particularly significant events. Focusing on one or two events does not mean ignoring all others. Instead, it means keeping a record of all events while selecting, elaborating, and analyzing one or two that represent an important development in perspective, goals, or plans. Thus the following format is designed to help you grow as a teacher by enabling you to benefit from your field experiences.

A. *Heading*

 Name: (This is unnecessary if you keep your logs in a bound notebook.)

 Date of field experiences reported: (A log entry should cover only one day and should be written the day of the experience. Otherwise memories tend to fade.)

 Time spent: (e.g., 1:30–3:00 P.M.)

B. *Sequence of events*

 Make a brief *list* describing what happened. By making a list, you keep a record of what happened. This record may be useful for future reference. It allows you to mention all events, even those that seemed insignificant to you at the time.

C. *Elaboration of one or two significant episodes*

 An episode is an ''event or sequence of events complete in itself but forming part of a larger one.''[21] *Select* one or two episodes that are significant to you. An episode may be significant because what happened bothers you, excites you, causes you to rethink your initial ideas (i.e., your perspective, goals, or plans), or convinces you that your initial ideas were valid. Therefore, whether the episodes reflect your successes or your failures, they are significant if you learned something important from them.

 Once you have selected one or two significant episodes, you should *describe* them in detail. When you describe the episodes, try to relive them. Reliving the experience will enable you to think about what you felt during the episode, how you perceived the responses of learners and other people (e.g., the cooperating teacher) to your actions and words, and who or what contributed significantly to shaping the events. This type of reflection will provide you with material for further reflection in the next section of the log.

D. *Analysis of episode(s)*

An analysis of episodes includes a description of why they were significant to you and how you interpret them. Try to figure out what you accomplished, identify problems that emerge and how you plan to follow up, and distill from the episodes what you learned. This last point is the most important. You may have learned what works in this situation and what does not. If so, describe what you conclude. But you may also have learned something about your philosophy of teaching (your perspective). Does the episode confirm your ideas or force you to reconsider them? Maybe some initial ideas you held rather dogmatically depend, to a large extent, on the situation in which you apply them. If so, what was it about the situation that affected the applicability of the ideas? Many experiences raise more questions than they answer. You might use your logs as an opportunity to note questions that arise during your field experiences which you want to discuss with your supervisor or bring up at a field experience seminar.

By reading some actual logs written by my students, you may get a clearer idea of how a log looks and what you might include in your own.

Sample Log 1 (A tutoring session with an eighth-grade girl living in a group home)

Log for March 15
Sequence of Events:

- Waited for Kim
- Worked on social studies assignment
- Was interrupted when the 8 o'clock end of study hour took over

Episodes:
The subject matter, even though we used social studies instead of math, showed little difference in the way Kim approaches school. So instead of relating this to our discussion and homework, I'll concentrate on Kim's attitudes. Tonight, I was presented with a serious problem because Kim definitely had no interest in understanding the terms which she was looking up to record their definitions. She wanted to accomplish her homework in a mechanical way and actually shunned my first attempts to offer meaning to her dictionarylike convoluted definitions. She drew away from my help,

saying that she couldn't handle trying to understand all these terms about government. I could see the stress and agony which she felt at the thought of doing this. Then she followed with her logic as to why she wanted to do the homework. It is quite interesting. She, first of all, stated that she didn't need to do this homework, that she could easily copy someone else's and get the same grade. But she didn't want to do this; she *wanted* to do her own homework and the reason for this was that she wanted the grade to be hers. Her honesty was an outcome of pride and the feeling of personal accomplishment. But the importance of understanding ideas, whether history or math, is altogether absent. If her learning processes were geared to understanding, it would take much more time. This would slow down her sense of accomplishment because she derives some satisfaction out of finishing her weekly assignment early and allowing some friends to copy it. She even said to me that she didn't want to understand the stuff, just to get it done.

Analysis:

I didn't know whether to question Kim's motives by confronting her. I'm in a position where I feel like less of an influence on Kim than her other teachers. I'm lacking the authority I would need to pressure Kim to alter her style because I think of the possible ways it could undermine Kim's views of her teachers. I'm also afraid that Kim would reject all the extra work, and myself with it. Her surroundings and patterns of living wouldn't be conducive to such a change. Further, her conceptions of school and its workings of grades and passing are so ingrained that I'm not sure my reasoning about the importance of understanding would be adequate to allow Kim to adopt this new outlook.

I don't think forcing Kim to change would improve her situation much because she's a fighter. But without any pressure she may never discover what is better for her before it is too late. I'm caught in the middle where I can force my help upon her and risk accomplishing nothing at best, or I can sit back and support any good signs of change and try for some accomplishment.

Tonight, I sat back and swallowed hard and lost the first few battles as Kim plugged away copying definitions out of the dictionary. I felt cheated for my time, disappointed in myself for not helping Kim at all but just accepting the way Kim wanted to do things. But as we or she progressed, I began to find points where she didn't understand a word and it gave me a chance to give her my version and supply some extra "everyday" type information. At the end, I was even able to sneak in a little lesson, but only because "The Great Compromise" isn't in the dictionary. So I felt like a losing string of battles was interrupted from time to time with a winning battle. So we did begin to accomplish a bit; I'm not too happy to accept this as much of a success.

Sample Log 2 (A primary grade science class)

Log for March 14 (no school on 3/11)
Events:
The first group of the K/1 class sat around one of the tables. I passed out a seed assortment and an egg carton to each child. They sorted the seeds. Each person got a paper cupful of soil and planted seeds that he/she wanted. The second group came in and we did the same thing with them.
Episode:
There is no real episode that sticks in my mind from today's work, but I was amused by the way that most of the kids sorted the seeds. Everyone, with the exception of Serena, separated the seeds one kind at a time. They would, for example, put all of the pinto beans each into its compartment and then go on to the next seed. I did not say anything, but I would've liked to grab a handful of seeds and put each one into its respective place. Serena did it "my way," but nobody else did.
Analysis:
After conducting today's session, I felt kind of bad because I really don't think there was too much of value for the students. The activity was proposed by the cooperating teacher and I thought it would be appropriate since I wanted to start a unit on plants and growing, in general.

Maybe sorting is an appropriate activity for that age level, but I think it was really shallow. I must say, though, that everyone was absorbed in the activity and once everyone had their plateful of seeds and egg carton, they were very well behaved and quiet. When it came time to do the watering, I let Danny, one of the more rambunctious persons, handle the watering can. I could sense that the cooperating teacher was a little leery of letting him do this (I was a little, too) but Danny was capable of doing his job and took pride in doing it ("you just need a little water").

I tried to work some more with Agate (or Agatka), the little Polish girl today. She was silent, as usual, but I spent some time with her. After class, I went to speak to her homeroom teacher to find out if Agate was receiving any individual instruction. In turns out that she had been, but it wasn't very successful. "I'm ready to give up on her." I thought to myself, "Good grief, the girl's only been in the U.S. for less than a month and here her teacher is about to give up on her."

Her teacher added that Agate has been "teasing" adults by laughing at them, but I could only get one specific incident out of her, and it didn't sound malicious at all to me. I went to talk to the principal to see if there was any way that I could work with Agate outside of the school situation to try and acquaint her with our society and our language. He called her father and said it was okay. I'm going to speak to her father tomorrow or Wednesday to see what we can arrange. I think that a less formal setting than the classroom may be a better place for Agate to learn, at least for now.

I'm scared. Mostly because I do not want to be rejected by this little girl, but partly because I do not know how to go about doing what I want to do. I'm not really sure exactly what it is that I want to do.

I know that she is interested in what is happening at school because her teacher said that she asks many questions of her father when she is at home at night. I must admit that I'd like to be the one that turns on the switch for Agate.

Sample Log 3 *(A third-grade science class)*

Log for March 31
Sequence of Events:

  I. Solo—Class by myself
 II. Organization.
    A. Girls—Write up experiment.
    B. Joel & Chris: Short writeup about crayfish. Label bones already assembled.
    C. Jeremy & Huck—Send messages in Morse code from sheets I had made up last week.
III. Clean up
IV. Second Graders:
    A. Mammals: Placentals vs. marsupials: pictures and slides on marsupials.

Episode:
This was the last day before release for spring recess for them. Everyone was edgy and preoccupied about going home and being off for a week. Still all in all, behavior was good even though I was the only one there. They usually only see me once a week. Because I had no classes, I was able to come on Thursday also. They seemed to like having science twice with me this week.

There was a reluctance among them to finish up their old projects and begin new ones. I don't think it was so much related to the fact that I wanted them to write up what they did as that they somehow felt "terminal" in my eyes. Joel and Chris seemed the most concerned about this. They both expressed a certain degree of anxiety about my leaving when my semester was over. They felt finishing up their projects was somehow terminating their relationship with me. I explained that, yes, I would be leaving when my semester was over, but that didn't mean they couldn't start new projects by themselves and continue them with someone else.

Analysis:

I was surprised at the degree of importance they had placed on my being there. A lot of their interest in their projects stemmed from the attention they were receiving from me. Both Joel and Chris seem to need a lot of adult interaction, both discipline and reassurance. Maybe their selection of *individual* projects was a way of assuring themselves of this personal attention. I've discovered just how fragile and flexible a child's ego can be. The problem now is going to be weaning them away from my attention and approval and making them less dependent upon such things. They have both come a long way though. Instead of doing bad things for attention, they seek approval for their actions and, more importantly, have discovered the values of *self*-esteem and *self*-motivation as a means of behavior modification. *They* control motives and actions.

Sample Log 4 *(A seventh-grade social studies class)*

Log for April 9
Episode:

I taught my first full class today! I planned the class and ran it, and Mrs. Thomas sat in the back in a student seat! I feel really up about the whole thing right now—I think I've finally gotten into some sort of stride now. The students were attentive, and asked questions like I couldn't believe. Even the so-called "problem students," the extremely antsy ones, were asking questions. Not just "What did you say? I didn't hear it," but good, solid "Why?" questions—the sort of questions that let me know I've gotten them thinking about the subject material.
Analysis:

I've been trying to figure out what it was about my teaching that got them to respond so well. Ahead of class, I had been anticipating problems because I had overheard teachers in the Social Studies Planning Office complaining about how poorly behaved all the students were. (There's a spaghetti dinner and the science fair tonight—I wish I could go, but unfortunately I have prior commitments.) I forced myself to assume they would behave, to give them only the admonition that I would take no more wisecracking or goofing off than Mrs. Thomas does. As it turned out, she beat me to the punch. She was called down to the office and left the class under my control completely until she got back. She warned them that she expected them to treat me with the same courtesy and respect they gave her, and that if she heard from me that they hadn't, she'd crack down on them harder than if they'd misbehaved for her. Now, I realize that gave me an unfair advantage over a teacher trying to make herself a controlling factor in a class on her own, but I was very relieved; it took my mind somewhat off of the one worry, and I was able to concentrate on the matter at hand—getting them enthusiastic about the Erie Canal.

"Discipline," or better, keeping control in the classroom, is not an easy thing in general. As I said, I got lucky today. I had students who *started out* concerned about doing what I said. So I was quickly able to get into the subject matter. Beyond that, though, I got them hooked. Judging by the number of hands up, the lack of whispering going on, the number of grins on students answering, and the scowls on students when someone gave the answer they were going to give, I think today's lesson was one they are going to remember. Each one of them had a chance to say something—ask a question, or try to answer one. I believe I didn't miss any.

I was very impressed with the level of thought in their answers as well as their questions. For example, after I had explained where the Erie Canal hooked up, I asked them what sort of goods might be coming up the Hudson River to farmers in middle New York. They got the guns and machinery I was aiming for, but they also thought of spices, fancy cloth, and goods from Europe, which *I* hadn't considered. They were drawing on lessons they had already had, which serves to reinforce the old knowledge at the same time it gives the new something to "attach" to.

I was able to cover most of my lesson plan, even mostly in the same order in which I had originally written it up. There was a little confusion at one point, when Mrs. Thomas joined in explaining aqueducts, and we suddenly realized that we weren't sure how it was spelled. Momentary confusion only—she had a dictionary sitting on the corner of her desk. I guess looking at the positive side of that, we just reminded them that learning never stops. If one of the students forgets how to spell a word, he or she might hesitate less about going to the dictionary than before—after all, the teacher looked up a spelling in class!

On a similar note, I also was able to give the library a plug. I mentioned briefly at the beginning of class how I'd gotten the book I would be showing them pictures out of. Even if in passing, they were reminded again that the library can be very helpful. They're already learning this maybe more than I did in my school, through the research project they are doing. This morning I was at the college library again, getting the latest requests copied off of microfilm. This time I got a set of interesting "extras" for the students who haven't gotten their act together yet. Boy, did Fred look like he felt important Monday when he had enough articles there to supply four other people with! Amazing, too, how that will probably encourage him to get things done early in the future—getting it done on time set him up for a lot of attention from his friends.

All in all, it was a pretty neat day! I wished, as I often have, that I didn't have the 3:00 commitment on Thursdays, so that I could stay for the ninth-period class as well. I'm to call Mrs. Thomas and discuss how the teaching went, and arrange getting together over their coming spring break. I won't be directly teaching, but Mrs. Thomas is going to let me help with the administrative garbage (details) that needs to get done. The immediately obvious one is compiling the students' individual presentations into group presentations. I'm actually quite looking forward to it—I'm getting to like Mrs. Thomas very much.

Sample Log 5 *(Tutoring a high school student in "life sciences")*

Log for February 17, 2:30–4:15
Events:

We went over her old notes, homework, quizzes, and tests, looking for the relationship between them. We also talked about her lab work and how she liked that aspect of the course. We then shifted our attention to the textbook and worked about halfway through Chapter 1.
Episode:

When I talked to Anne's teacher and his assistant, they both felt her main problem was attention and motivation. Perhaps that is why I so easily noticed the former problem today. I realize it was a Friday afternoon and few people are into schoolwork at that point, but it was still amazing how quick her attention would wander.

We were working in the school library, trying to pull the central meaning out of the text sections. For instance, we would read the section on bacteria characteristics and then try to make an outline, but she wasn't really there. I don't wish to exaggerate this because she was paying some attention though I felt it wasn't much. I felt annoyed, but I also felt anxious because I might be just boring and not teaching "right." This is really the first teaching I've done dealing with an academic subject and consequently I am in need of improvement.
Analysis:

I can't truthfully say I gave any solution to this problem or that I had previously thought about it. I just assumed we would work on the material and on "understanding type problems." Understanding is not the main problem; bringing attention to the subject is. At first glance through her biology book I thought, at the risk of sounding arrogant, that it was so basic that even people who are not considered smart could work through it. But I'm beginning to see that I was really off the mark as to the problem. One reason this is so interesting to me is because it sounds somewhat like myself in high school. Attention is something both Anne and I have a problem with, but in my case I rely on my relatively good learning ability. Anne can't. I don't see how to change her attitude or even if it is my responsibility or right, but I do think her attention can be worked on.

NOTES

1. John Dewey, *How We Think: A Restatement of the Relation of Reflective Thinking to the Educative Process* (Boston: D.C. Heath, 1933), p. 3.
1. Ibid., p. 17.
3. Ibid.
4. Carl Grant and Kenneth Zeichner, "On Becoming a Reflective Teacher," in *Preparing for Reflective Teaching*, ed. Carl A. Grant (Boston: Allyn and Bacon, 1984), p. 4.
5. Ibid.
6. I am indebted to Grant and Zeichner (ibid.) for the main points of this section.
7. Philip Jackson, *Life in Classrooms* (New York: Holt, Rinehart and Winston, 1968).
8. Ibid., pp. 11–12.
9. Ibid., p. 13.
10. Grant and Zeichner, op. cit., p. 9.
11. Jackson, op. cit., pp. 151–152.
12. Ibid., p. 151 (italics in original).
13. Grant and Zeichner, op. cit., p. 10.
14. Ibid., p. 10.
15. Ibid., p. 11.
16. Wayne Hoy and William Rees, "The Bureaucratic Socialization of Student Teachers," *Journal of Teacher Education* 28 (Jan.–Feb. 1977), pp. 23–26.
17. Ibid., p. 11.
18. Walter Doyle and Gerald Ponder, "The Ethic of Practicality: Implications for Curriculum Development," in *Curriculum Theory*, ed. Alex Molnar and John Zahorik (Washington, D.C.: Association for Supervision and Curriculum Development, 1977).
19. John Goodlad and Frances Klein, *Behind the Classroom Door* (Washington, Ohio: Jones Publishing, 1970).
20. Rob Walker and Clem Adelman, *A Guide to Classroom Observation* (London: Methuen, 1975), p. 18.
21. *Webster's New World Dictionary of the American Language*, Second College Edition, (Englewood Cliffs, N.J.: Prentice-Hall, 1970), p. 471.

PART 2
Situation Analysis

CHAPTER 4

What Is the Situation in the School and the Community?

Most people approach social situations with caution. They reserve judgment and commitment until they know something about the individuals and their expectations, the social rules and procedures, and the relation between the specific situation and the larger social context. Most of these factors can be taken for granted in familiar settings, such as college courses or meetings of student activity groups, though every new course or meeting requires a bit of analysis and readjustment. For example, most students spend their first class session figuring out what their instructor expects of the students. And most freshmen in college spend the entire year figuring out how the whole place works both academically and socially.

In other words, some sort of situation analysis is a necessary part of any social interaction. Since a field experience in teaching is one sort of social interaction, it, too, requires some preliminary analysis of the setting.

This chapter and the next use two types of information for the purpose of analysis: observations and conversations. Observations can focus on any of the following: (1) the community or neighborhood in which you have your field experiences, (2) the particular school agency or institution, including the physical, social, and personal setting, (3) the room, home, or more generally the space in which you work, (4) the cooperating teacher (CT) or co-worker, if any, including his or her lessons. In addition to observations, conversations with any of the following people could be informative: the CT or co-workers (if any), the principal or immediate supervisor of your work (if any), and the learners, clients, or members of the group or family.

If your field experience is done within a school or as a supplement to schooling (e.g., tutoring in school subjects), then you might focus your analysis on the school, the student population, the community, the cooperating teacher, and the classroom. On the other hand, if your field experience is done within another context (e.g., a 4-H club or a correctional facility), you will have to adapt Chapters 4 and 5 to the special setting in which you will teach. In doing so, you will find ideas in these two chapters that you can modify for your purposes. For example, if you serve as a co-leader of 4-H, the other co-leader is not a cooperating teacher (CT) but much of what we discuss about CTs applies equally well to co-leaders.

This chapter focuses only on the analysis of the school, the community, and the general student population. The next chapter examines the cooperating teacher, the classroom, and the students in a specific classroom.

THE COMMUNITY

The classroom is a society in miniature. This minisociety reflects in part the society in which the school exists. Children often act and interact in certain ways because they see their parents and friends do so. If they experience anti-intellectualism, materialism, conformity, or prejudice at home or at their neighbors' houses, they are likely to demonstrate these tendencies at school. If their parents and neighbors support the school's efforts, place a high priority on achievement, and are courteous and well-mannered, the children are likely to be similarly inclined in school. It is therefore important to find out about the community from which the learners come and in which the school is situated. Although interviews with parents and community members are obviously desirable, they are typically not feasible.

EXERCISE 4.1   Analysis of the Community

Here are some things you can do to learn about the community:

1. Read a local newspaper every day for a couple of weeks. Pay particular attention to news stories, editorials and letters to the editor concerning the schools.
   a. Is the community proud of its schools? What do they seem to be most proud of? The athletic teams? The band? Scholarship winners? Innovations? Efforts to cut the budget? Improved test scores? The buildings?

   ▶

   b. What makes people angry? Liberal policies? Conservative policies? Indecision? Political heavy-handedness? Permissiveness? Vandalism?

▶

c. Read non-education-related items. How diverse is the community? Ethnically? In terms of socioeconomic status?

▶

d. Where do people work and what do they spend their leisure time doing?

▶

Write a brief description of the community and its attitude toward the schools as reflected by the newspaper.

▶

2. Walk around the neighborhood of the school, looking at the houses, businesses, and people on the street. Go to a local establishment near the school building, perhaps a barber shop, restaurant, bar, or laundromat. If asked about yourself, mention that you will be working at the school soon and note the reaction. Sympathy? Admiration? Suspicion? Listen to conversations, or start one. What do the people think about the job the schools are doing? What do they think about young people today? What is first and foremost on their minds? Property taxes? Deterioration of the neighborhood? Permissiveness? Vandalism? Busing? Write a brief description of the neighborhood, its inhabitants, and their attitude toward the schools as you find it reflected in these experiences.

▶

Compare your two descriptions. Do they conflict or do they complement one another? If they conflict, how can you reconcile them? Does the newspaper really reflect the local neighborhood? Did you read enough of it? Were you exposed to enough community members to get an accurate picture?

▶

Now try to draw some implications from this study for the school and classroom. To do this, make some predictions of what you might find in the school. What sorts of careers are likely to be most and least highly prized? How much value is likely to be placed on proper dress for the pupils and for the teachers? How cautious are the teachers likely to be with regard to discussing controversial issues in the classroom? How much support from the parents are teachers likely to get when they discipline students?

▶

THE SCHOOL

Schools are both similar and different. Compared with hospitals and churches, schools in general are distinctive and highly uniform. But within this relative uniformity, there are significant differences or variations on a theme. And just as with faces, the more one comes to know schools, the more one becomes sensitive to the differences. Some teem with activity. Others are as hushed as libraries. Some are colorful and stimulate the senses. Others are dull and drab. In some, long, straight corridors dominate the architecture. In others, open spaces are common. Some school grounds resemble country clubs while others resemble prisons. What accounts for the differences in atmosphere and what effect do these differences have on the people that function there?

EXERCISE 4.2   A Walk Around the School

Take a walk around the school, both inside and out (remember to have the permission of the principal). Here are some things to which you might want to pay particular attention:

1. *The halls.* Who is in the halls during class time? Teachers? The principal? Students? Do the students you find have hall passes? Where are they going?

▶

Look at the walls. Are they used for displays of any kind? If so, is it student work? Commercially prepared displays? Are they at eye level for children? What subject matter is represented? Any announcements or bulletin boards? What is on them?

▶

What is the noise level and what kind of noise is it? Laughter? Yelling? A "hum of activity"? Hammering and other construction noises? Teachers' voices?

▶

Are the halls littered? How much pride in the school is evidenced?

▶

2. *The library (learning center).* Is it an inviting place? Do you find it a comfortable environment for reading? Browsing?

What is the noise level? Hushed silence? Outbursts of laughter? Are there distractions?

Is the atmosphere serious or silly? Stiff or relaxed?

What is the attitude of the teacher in charge? Does he or she act more as a resource person or as a warden?

Are students there by choice or by assignment? Do they come with or without passes? Is coming to the library viewed more as a privilege or as a necessary task?

▶

EXERCISE 4.3   A Conversation with the Principal

You might get an opportunity to talk with the principal. If you do, here are some suggestions that will increase your understanding of the school and, particularly, the principal's role in it.

Curriculum.

Ask the principal about the school's objectives and curriculum. Is there a state curriculum? Try to acquire a copy. Under what objectives does the school operate? Are there objectives that the school as a whole tries to achieve? Are there particular objectives for each grade level and/or each subject? How and by whom were these developed? Who selected the textbooks and programs in use? How were they selected?

▶

Rules and Discipline.

What are the school's rules and how is discipline handled? Is there a printed set of rules of conduct? If not, what are they? What infractions are the most serious and what are the penalties? What is the frequency of infractions? Who is supposed to deal with each type of infraction? When should an infraction be handled entirely within the classroom? When and how should the principal (or vice-principal) be involved? When and how should parents be involved?

▶

Leadership Style.

Try to determine from the principal's remarks if he or she is more of a manager or an instructional leader. The former tries to keep a school running smoothly and efficiently. The latter tries to stimulate innovation, to encourage thought and debate, to keep teachers' minds active, and even to set an example as a continuously growing and expanding professional. Obviously the two types of principals have very different approaches to controversy, disruptions, noise, etc. Clearly, the kind of teacher you are encouraged to be will differ depending upon the atmosphere established by different principals.

▶

EXERCISE 4.4   A Visit to the Faculty Room

If you go to the faculty room for a cup of coffee, listen to the types of conversations going on. Here are some things to notice: How old are the teachers in the room? What subjects are discussed? Are they related or not related to school? What outside activities predominate? Sports? Politics? Social events? What school-related matters predominate? Classroom problems? Concern for particular pupils? The administration? Other teachers? Parents? School sports? When discussion is on a particular student, does the talk reflect disgust, respect, hope, or despair for the student? How do the teachers dress?

▶

At this point it might be worthwhile to summarize your conclusions about the school and its staff. What is their philosophy of teaching? Do you agree with it? What sorts of problems might you encounter working there?

▶

THE STUDENTS IN THE SCHOOL

By studying the students in the school, you can find out the composition of the student population and what it is like being a student in this school. These two aspects of school life are best identified through a combination of talks with and observations of the students. Here are some suggestions.

EXERCISE 4.5   Conversations with Students

During recesses, lunchtime, or after school, try to talk with at least one student. You might tell the student that you are not reporting any information to anybody, that you just want to find out about the school in which you will be working.

You might ask about the student's neighborhood. Are the people there like the people in the school? How are they different?

What does the student want to do after leaving school? Has he or she made any plans? If the student is old enough, ask if he or she works after school hours or during vacations.

Does the student like school? What about it does he or she like and dislike? What is the student's favorite subject? What about it does he or she like? Ask similar questions about the subject the student dislikes the most and the subject in which the student does the best and the worst. What about extracurricular activities, including sports?

Who is the student's favorite teacher this year? Who is the favorite teacher of all time? Would most others agree? What makes this teacher the best? You might try to identify the characteristics of this student's "ideal" teacher.

Who are this student's friends? Is this student in a clique? If so, what is it like? Who in the school does he or she like or dislike? What does he or she like or dislike about these kids? Whose opinion really counts?

Are there kids in the school that are very "different"? What makes them "different"? How does this student feel about kids that are "different"?

How much help does this student receive from his or her parents? What kind of help? With homework or projects? Moral support? Has this student ever been in trouble in school? What kind? How did the parents react?

After talking to a few students, try to summarize your notes here, comparing and contrasting the students' backgrounds, goals and aspirations, likes and dislikes, ideal teacher, friendship groups, attitudes about people who are "different," and the role of their parents in their schooling.

▶ *Backgrounds:*

▶ *Goals and aspirations:*

▶ *Likes and dislikes*

▶ *Ideal teacher:*

▶ *Friendship groups and "significant others":*

Attitudes about people who are "different":

▶

Parents' role:

▶

EXERCISE 4.6   Observing Students

You might also try to observe some students. The cafeteria during lunch and the playground or school grounds during recess are possible places.

Dress. How are the children dressed? Comment on neatness and apparent affluence. Also note differences in dress among groups of children.

Language. What is their out-of-class language like? How is it different from their in-class language? What sorts of emotions do they express with their language? Do they use abusive language? Note differences in languages among groups of children.

Interests. If you are unobtrusive, you will be able to overhear fragments of conversations. What do the children talk about? Teachers? Sports and cars? Grades? The opposite sex? Clothes? Current events? Tests? Note differences in topics of conversation for different groups.

Groups. What groups can you identify? (Groups are particularly noticeable in secondary schools.) Some groups you might notice are "jocks," "druggies," "straights," "punks," "nerds," "preppies," and students of various racial or ethnic backgrounds. How would you characterize each group? Consider dress, language, interests, how physical, materialistic, and so on. How rigid is group definition? That is, are some students members of more than one group? Or do some members of groups at least mix with members of other groups? Are there loners? What are their characteristics?

Territory. Does each of the groups have its own "territory"? Which one has the most territory? The least territory? How closely guarded is each group's territory?

Conflict. What sorts of conflict do you observe? Are the protagonists members of different groups? What is the source of the conflict (e.g., physical or verbal abuse, invasion of one group's territory by another)? How is the conflict settled (if at all) and by whom?

Dominance and Power. Do any of the groups appear to be dominant? Which are the most and the least powerful groups? What is the source of each group's power (e.g., academic skills, athletic skill, muscle, "street knowledge")? Do any of the groups depend on adult approval for their power?

Summarize what you have found about the students in the school. Who are they and what is it like to "live" in this school?

CHAPTER 5

What Is the Situation with the Cooperating Teacher and the Classroom?

Probably the greatest influence on the quality of a field experience, particularly for the student teacher, is the cooperating teacher. In a sense, the student teacher is an apprentice and the cooperating teacher is a master teacher. Even in many less-formal arrangements such as exploratory field experiences, there is a cooperating teacher on whom the success of the field experience depends. Cooperating teachers always do some things that the student teacher disagrees with or does not understand. The purpose of this chapter is not to persuade you that the cooperating teacher knows best, but instead to help you understand how the cooperating teacher views teaching, to help you see the situation through his or her eyes.

As Lortie[1] mentions, "the average student has spent 13,000 hours in direct contact with classroom teachers by the time he or she graduates from high school."[2] Lortie calls this contact "apprenticeship by observation."[3] There are definite limits to this type of apprenticeship, however.

> The student is the "target" of teacher efforts and sees the teacher front stage and center like an audience viewing a play. Students do not receive invitations to watch the teacher's performance from the wings; they are not privy to the teacher's private intentions and personal reflections on classroom events. Students rarely participate in selecting goals, making preparations, or postmortem analyses. Thus they are not pressed to place the teacher's actions in a pedagogically oriented framework. They are witnesses from their own student-oriented perspectives. . . . What students learn about teaching, then, is intuitive and imitative rather than

explicit and analytical; it is based on individual personalities rather than pedagogical principles.[4]

Students, then, should be expected to know no more about teaching than an avid moviegoer knows about directing or a dance buff knows about choreography. One of the tasks of this chapter will be to unlearn (but not to forget) the student pespective as one step toward becoming a teacher. As Walker and Adelman[5] state:

> The teacher sees the class quite differently from the way it is seen by a child. Children are faced with the problem of either producing a perform- ance that the teacher requires, or reacting against it in some way. In either event, a major element in the classroom situation for the pupils is what they take to be the demands of the teacher whether these are stated or unstated. For them the situation is inevitably one of constraint. . . .
>
> For the teacher the problem is quite different: his task is to get beyond the constraints as rapidly as possible; he has to define the situation and set the pace—to make sure that what he wants to happen seems to happen.
>
> For many people starting teaching, it comes as shock to realize that the spotlight is on them, that the initiative is in their hands, that they suddenly have responsibility for what happens, what will happen and what might happen. The classroom, which they saw previously as an unshakeable social structure, suddenly becomes bewildering and problematic, fraught with difficulties at every turn. Many consequently exaggerate in their minds the degree to which the situation is "out of control" simply be- cause they are unaware of the change in perspective brought about by the shift from the back to the front of the class.[6]

Thus seeing the teacher and the classroom differently is the main task here. Whereas the last chapter focused on the school as a whole, this chap- ter examines the particular classroom or setting in which you will work. Whereas the last chapter helped you to see the school from the faculty's, the principal's, and the typical student's perspective, this chapter helps you understand what dilemmas and tasks the teacher faces and what the teacher does to cope with them. The chapter concludes with a look at the particular students you will be teaching.

THE CLASSROOM

Teachers try to provide environments for learning. The environment in- cludes a physical and an interpersonal dimension. In order to understand the resources and constraints within which the classroom operates and the way the classroom layout reflects the teacher's personal perspective, we will begin our analysis of the classroom by examining the physical layout.

EXERCISE 5.1   Classroom Map

One way to analyze the classroom layout is to make a sketch of the classroom, roughly to scale. Here are some things to include and label, if present:

1. Doors and windows
2. Desks, tables, and chairs
3. Bookcases, cabinets, and display cases
4. Closets and other storage areas
5. Sinks and lavatories
6. Adjoining rooms or hallways
7. Blackboards, projectors, screens
8. Special resource areas (e.g., math table, reading corner)

(Use a separate sheet of paper for your map.)

▶

In addition, you might want to note the following features of the classroom:

1. *Walls.* Describe color. What posters, pictures, wall charts, exhibits, notices are there? How long have they been there? Do they look as though they are still being used by someone?
2. *Vantage Point.* Do any other parts of the school overlook the room? Does the room look out on the outside world?
3. *Furniture.* Does the furniture arrangement appear more conducive to cooperative, competitive, or individualistic work? How flexible does the arrangement appear? In what condition is the furniture? Has it been abused?
4. *Equipment.* What kinds of equipment are there? How accessible is it? What condition is it in? Does it look as though it is seldom, occasionally, or frequently used? And used by whom, the teacher or the learners?
5. *Bulletin Boards.* What are they used for? Who uses them (the teacher, the learners or the administration)? How recently were they changed?
6. *Specialization.* Are there areas in the room used for special purposes? Is specialization by school subject (e.g., math area), by topic or unit (e.g., space travel), or by learning mode (e.g., audiotutorial)?
7. *Atmosphere.* Note the room's temperature, air circulation and ventilation, smells, lighting (artificial and natural) and glare, acoustics (echoes and resonance), outside noise (e.g., traffic), and furniture noise.

General comments: What are your general impressions of this room? Is it crowded, cluttered, or comfortable? Is it boring and bland, or stimulating? How would you like to spend six hours a day here? If you had not met or observed the teacher, from what you have noted about the classroom, what might you assume about the teacher's approach to teaching?

▶

EXERCISE 5.2   Lesson profile[7]

Like a piece of music, a good lesson can have different "movements" which have various, contrasting moods but which, taken together as a sequence, form a cumulative experience.[8]

With this basic familiarity of the classroom layout, you are equipped to observe the class in action. A useful way to begin is by making a lesson profile of one or two lessons (i.e., class periods). Think of a lesson as a sequence of events; there is a beginning, a middle, and an end. The beginning might consist of a settling-down period, a preface and/or introduction, or the presentation of instructions for the main activity. The middle might entail a demonstration, lecture, film, discussion, presentation of work by groups, set work, or any combination of these and other activities. The end might be used as a period for summary, conclusions, cleaning up, homework assignment, test taking, among other things. You might list the sequence of events that took place during the lesson, indicating the approximate length of time each event required, and describing what seem to you to be important aspects of each. You might want to include information about some of the following for each event:

1. Activity of teacher (what is the teacher doing?)
2. Activity of learners (what are the learners doing?)
3. Resources (what resources are utilized?)
4. Noise level (high, moderate, low)
5. Use of space (what regions of the classroom are used?)
6. Concentration level (high, moderate, low)
7. Movement of learners
8. Movement of teacher
9. Number of learners involved
10. Lines of communication (teacher-to-student, student-to-teacher, student-to-student)

There are, of course, other aspects you might want to use. Feel free to improvise. (Use a separate sheet of paper for your lesson profile.)

After completing a lesson profile, consider asking to see the cooperating teacher's lesson plan, if one exists. Compare the plan with the profile.

What, if any, tentative conclusions do you have regarding this teacher's perspective? For example:

1. How responsive does the teacher appear to be to moods or interests of the learners? To what extent does any discrepancy between the lesson plan and profile represent responsiveness of the cooperating teacher?
2. Does the cooperating teacher treat different learners differently in terms of grouping, time allocation, tasks, standards, etc.?
3. How much of the lesson is done by learners individually and how much in groups? Is there a spirit of competition or cooperation in the groups? Does the cooperating teacher say or do anything to encourage or discourage this spirit?
4. How formal/informal does the cooperating teacher appear? What does the cooperating teacher do to develop or reinforce this role?
5. What seems to be the point of the lesson? For example, is it to memorize some material, share some ideas, find some "correct" answers or procedures, check to see if the learners have been doing their work, clarify ideas? How does the cooperating teacher communicate the intent to the class?

EXERCISE 5.3   Analysis of Lesson Elements

You can take your observation of the lesson one step further by applying a template to the lesson, that is, looking for a set of basic elements of the lesson. For our present purposes we will consider a relatively simple and straightforward approach to the analysis of lessons, adapted from the work of Hunter.[9] Hunter provides an outline of the basic elements of a lesson which can function as a set of questions to answer as you observe the teacher in action:

1. *Anticipatory set.* What has the teacher done to get the students' attention, to relate the lesson to what the students have done previously, and to engage them in the lesson? Look for how the teacher communicates to students that the lesson is about to begin, whether the teacher reviews previous lessons, how the teacher tries to stimulate interest, and what the teacher does to lay the groundwork for the lesson.

2. *Objective and purpose.* What has the teacher done to communicate to the students what they are supposed to get out of the lesson and why that is important?

▶

3. *Input.* What knowledge and skills necessary to achieve the lesson's objective does the teacher make available to the students and how does the teacher provide them? Look for the specific methods employed, whether they include lecture, discussion, laboratory, seatwork, or some other method.

▶

4. *Modeling.* How does the teacher show the students what they are expected to produce or learn to do? What kinds of examples and demonstrations are employed?

▶

5. *Checking for understanding.* How does the teacher monitor the students' understanding of concepts and proficiency in skills during the lesson? How does the teacher adjust the lesson on the basis of this feedback? Look for the ways in which the teacher invites questions, how the teacher asks and answers questions (including the amount of time the teacher waits for an answer), how many and what type of students the teacher involves in questioning, and what the teacher does with a student's answer, especially when it is wrong.

▶

6. *Guided practice.* How does the teacher give the students opportunities to practice using their new knowledge or skill under direct teacher supervision?

▶

7. *Independent practice.* How does the teacher provide opportunities for students to practice using their new knowledge or skills independently after the teacher is reasonably sure that students will not make serious errors?

▶

As Hunter points out, a common error in the observation of teaching is the belief that "all good things must be in every lesson."[10] The teacher must decide which of the elements to include, as well as how to include it. The advantage of templates like Hunter's is that they give us things to look for; the disadvantage is that the template is not appropriate for every lesson. Figuring out why particular elements are absent from a lesson can provide important insights into teaching in its own right.

EXERCISE 5.4   Conversation with the Teacher

If you can arrange one, a get-acquainted meeting with the cooperating teacher could prove informative.

One purpose of a conversation with the cooperating teacher is to find out the teacher's perspective on teaching and the beliefs underlying the teacher's actions. In order to meet this purpose, objectivity and suspension of judgment are important, even if you strongly disagree with what you hear.

There are many questions you might ask the cooperating teacher. I have organized a series of questions into a set of eight issues. Rather than try to cover all eight in the limited time you can reasonably expect the cooperating teacher to give you, you could select the two or three that interest you most. Your interests may derive from the amount of thought you have personally given to the issues or from the apparent significance of the issues to the cooperating teacher based on your classroom observations.

The eight issues are as follows (numbers in parentheses refer to the questions in the list following this one):

1. Control
   a. How are decisions made about teaching methods? (1,2,3,5,6,9,11)
   b. How are decisions made about curriculum and content? (4,5,9,10,11)
   c. How much and what kind of control should teachers have over pupils' behavior? (7,8,18)
2. Diversity
   a. What learner differences are significant, and should different types of learners be treated differently? (12)
3. Learning
   a. Is learning facilitated by a competitive or cooperative environment? (14)
   b. What is the basis of motivation? (14)
4. Teacher's Role
   a. How formal a role should the teacher assume? (13)
5. School and Society
   a. How active should a teacher become in political reform? (15)
   b. Should the school reflect the current society or attempt to reform it? (15)
6. Knowledge
   a. What should be the curriculum's emphasis (16,18)
   b. Should subject matters be kept separate or integrated? (17)
7. Rewards and Criteria
   a. What are the rewards of teaching? (19)
   b. What are the criteria by which teachers should be evaluated? (20,21)
8. CT–ST Relationship
   a. What should be the role of the student teacher? (22,23)

Try to select a time when the cooperating teacher is alone in the classroom or somewhere outside when distractions are minimal. Here are some suggestions for questions covering the eight issues above. You will probably have to modify them in your own meeting. Some of the questions might be best left until a future meeting, after you have established a better relationship with the cooperating teacher.

1. I've noticed some special areas in your room. (Specify one of them.) What do you and the kids do in this area? Who gets to use it? How are they selected? (Repeat for each area.)

2. Did you arrange the room this way? (If no): Who did? (If yes): What were you trying to do with this arrangement? How long has it been this way?

3. Did you put up the posters, pictures, exhibits, etc., on the walls and bulletin boards? (If no): Who did? (If yes): What was the purpose? When did you put them up? (May be different for each poster.)

4. I've been looking through the textbook. How was it selected and by whom? How do you like it? What are its strengths? Weaknesses? Is it successful with some kids but not with others? (Repeat this set of questions for each text.)

5. I also looked over the worksheets, labs, and/or quizzes you've been using. Did you write them? (If no): Where did you get them? (If yes): When did you make them up? Did you base them on anything in particular? Are you happy with them?

6. I enjoyed the lesson(s) (or classes) that I had the opportunity to observe. When I compared your lesson plan with the actual lesson, I noticed that you did not follow your plan precisely. (This question is used only if you noticed some discrepancies.) What caused you to modify your plan?

7. What rules do you expect the kids in your class to follow? (*Probe:* rules for waiting their turn to speak and to receive help, rules for moving around the classroom, leaving the classroom, being on time, what to do when finished with work, working together, resolving conflicts among kids, homework, forms to follow, procedures for work, language, noises, who may speak, etc.) Does the school have rules or regulations with which you disagree? (If yes): Why do you disagree? Do you follow them anyway? Which rules are the most important to you? How do you handle infractions? Are there some kids that break rules more than other kids? Tell me about those kids.

8. How do you enforce your rules? What happens when someone breaks one? Does it depend upon who that kid is? Do you ever feel that you are losing control of the class? How do you go about regaining control?

9. Do parents ever visit the classroom? (If no): Would you like them to? (If yes): Are you pleased that they do? How can parents be of most help to you as a teacher? How can they hinder you? Should parents be involved in selection of school books? What about in hiring teachers?

10. Does the school or the district have a curriculum? Are you expected to follow it? Do you? Did you have any say in it? Do you ever depart from it?

11. Do your students' (or "children's," for primary grades) interests affect your teaching methods? (If yes): In what ways? Do their interests affect the content? Do they have any say in what they study? (If yes): In what ways?

12. What sorts of students do you teach? Are there different groups? Could you describe the groups? Do you devote more time to certain students? Do you expect all of them to assume the same degree of responsibility for their learning? Do you use different criteria to evaluate different students? Do you find the diversity among them to be a major problem?

13. How friendly are you with the children? Do you tell them much about yourself? What do you think is the proper role for a teacher?

14. Do you try to develop a sense of competition in your class? How important is cooperating among the kids? What do you use to motivate the kids? (*Probe:* grades, interest and curiosity, comparison of one child's work with another's, fear.)

15. Do you ever let the kids know your political views? Do you think that the schools are doing a pretty good job or do they need to change drastically? Are you trying to help kids fit into the society as it is, or would you like to equip them to reform society?

16. How important are the *3 Rs* to you? What about the children's emotional needs? Are they important? What about things like problem-solving skills and creativity—are they important? What is the relative importance of these various goals?

17. Do you ever try to relate one subject matter (e.g., science) with another that you or another teacher teaches? Or do you think different subject matters should be treated separately?

18. What do you test for? How important are your tests and quizzes?

19. Most people have days in their work when they go home feeling especially good because the day and its activities were particularly rewarding. What makes a good day in teaching for you?

20. How do you tell how well you are doing as a teacher? That is, what things provide you with evidence that you're doing a good job?

21. Suppose you accidentally happened to overhear a group of your former students discussing you as a teacher. What kinds of things would you like to hear them saying?

22. Why did you ask to have a student teacher (or aide, depending upon your role)?

23. What do you expect from me?

On the following Teacher Analysis Form, you can summarize the cooperating teacher's responses in column 3 for each issue (expressed as a general question in column 1). The number of the question sets which correspond to the issue are listed in column 2.

FORM 5.1 TEACHER ANALYSIS FORM

(1)	(2)	(3)
Issue	**Question Set Number**	

1. *Control*
   a. How are decisions made about teaching
      1. Special areas
      2. Room arrangement
      3. Posters, pictures, etc.
      5. Worksheets/labs/quizzes
      6. Modification of lesson plan
      9. Parents visiting classrooms
      11. Student interest affecting teaching methods

   b. How are decisions made about curriculum and content?
      4. Textbook(s)
      5. Worksheets/labs/quizzes
      9. Parents visiting classrooms
      10. School curriculum
      11. Student interest affecting teaching methods

   c. How much and what kind of control should teachers have over pupils' behavior?
      7. Rules/regulations
      18. Enforcement of rules
      18. Tests

2. *Diversity*
   a. What pupil differences are significant and should different pupils be treated differently?
      12. Groups of children and their treatment

3. *Learning*
   a. Is learning facilitated by a competitive or cooperative environment?
      14. Competition/cooperation/motivaton of students

   b. What is the basis for motivation?
      14. Competition/cooperation/motivation of students

4. *Teacher's Role*
   a. How formal a role should the teacher assume in the classroom?
      13. Teacher's personal relationship with students

5. *School and Society*
   a. How active should the teacher become in political reform?
      15. Political views and reform

(1)	(2)	(3)
Issue	**Question Set Number**	

b. Should the school reflect the current society or attempt to reform it? 15. Political views and reform

6. *Knowledge* 16. *3 R's,* emotional needs, etc.
   a. What should be the curriculum's emphasis? 18. Areas tested
   b. Should subject matters be kept separate or integrated? 17. Separate subject matters

7. *Rewards and Criteria* 19. Good days
   a. What are the rewards of teaching?
   b. What are the criteria by which teachers should be evaluated? 20. Doing a good job
   21. Overhearing students

8. *CT–ST Relationship* 22. Reason for having an ST
   a. What should be the role of the student teacher? 23. Expectations

---

THE STUDENTS

"Every person is unique." Although most teachers would agree with this statement, they tend to talk about student types—slow learners, underachievers, disadvantaged, science-oriented, jock, or college-bound. This tendency is understandable in all people when they try to reduce the complexity of a situation. This typing of students transforms a room filled with 35 unique individuals to one with 3, 5, or even 10 types of students. But however understandable or natural this tendency is, it is also potentially dangerous because such a practice might blind teachers to their students' individuality. This is why you should get to know your students as individuals. Each has particular strengths and weaknesses, likes and dislikes, and desirable and undesirable traits. Not only is each student an individual, but also each is a member of one or more friendship groups. Understanding who a student looks to for approval or respect is also of vital importance.

The first step in getting acquainted with the students is to observe them in class. Here is one approach to observing students:

EXERCISE 5.5   Who Are the Students?[11]

Stand as unobtrusively as possible in the classroom before any students arrive. Jot down notes as they begin to arrive. Some suggestions for your notes are as follows:

1. Notice who arrives first and last.
2. How many and what age and gender are the students in this class?
3. Do students remain in the same groups inside the classroom as those in which they arrived?
4. Look at the overall spacing between groups. Is it uniform? Does it reflect furniture or resource location or friendship groups? Are there any cliques?
5. Who are the isolates?
6. How much movement between groups occurs? Note how changes in groupings occur during the class period.
7. What roles do particular students play? For example, who is the joker, the cynic, the teacher's pet, the introvert, etc.
8. Which students raise their hands most often and least often (or never) when the teacher asks a question?
9. On which students does the teacher never call?
10. Is the behavior of the students who sit in the back of the room different from that of the rest of the class? What about the corners, the middle, and the front?
11. Which students seem to be paying most and least attention and what is the range of attention spans?
12. Which students asks for most help and whom do they ask (the teacher, nearby students)?
13. Which students receive the most praise and which receive the most criticism? Which students seem to be ignored?
14. Try to determine the extent of any division of labor in the class or within the groups. Are there different roles? Do all carry out the same tasks? Are roles and tasks fixed, or do they shift among students? Who seems to assign these roles or tasks? How smooth-running and cohesive is the class and is each group?
15. If there are groups, how much communication and sharing exists among them?
16. Is the relationship among the students mostly cooperative, competitive or individualistic? For example, when the teacher asks a student a question, do other students help the first student answer it, or do they try to answer it themselves?
17. On which students does the teacher rely to help decide when to move on. When teachers decide to move on to another activity or topic, they commonly base this decision on their judgment that certain students have "got-

ten'' the material. This group of students has been termed the "steering group."[12] Where do they stand in relation to the rest of the class in terms of ability?

Summarize your observations of the students in the classroom. What are the prominent groups and how do the groups interact? Which individuals play key roles in relations among students and in terms of the lesson flow?

▶

NOTES

1. Dan Lortie, *Schoolteacher* (Chicago: University of Chicago Press, 1975).
2. Ibid., p. 61.
3. Ibid., p. 61.
4. Ibid., p. 62.
5. Rob Walker and Clem Adelman, *A Guide to Classroom Observation* (London: Methuen, 1975).
6. Ibid., p. 8.
7. Adapted from Walker and Adelman, op. cit.
8. Ibid., p. 25.
9. Madeline Hunter, "Knowing, Teaching and Supervising," in *Using What We Know About Teaching,* ed. Philip Hosford (Alexandria, Va.: Association for Supervision and Curriculum Development, 1984), pp. 169–192.
10. Ibid., p. 176.
11. Adapted from Walker and Adelman, op. cit.
12. Urban Dahllof, *Ability Grouping, Content Validity and Curriculum Process Analysis* (New York: Columbia University, Teachers College Press, 1971).

PART 3
Search for a Perspective

CHAPTER 6

How Do Your Experiences as a Learner and Teacher Contribute to Your Perspective?

No one's mind is empty. This statement of the obvious applies to the novice as well as to the expert. We have ideas and ideals about such things as parenting, marriage, coaching, and appropriate bedside manner, even though we may never have been an official parent, spouse, coach, or doctor. The same can be said of teaching. We all have some beliefs about what good teaching is, whether or not we have official status as a "teacher."

Our own beliefs, principles, and ideals (termed "perspective"), however unexamined or incomplete they may now be, function for each of us as a personal "platform." They justify and unify our decisions and actions (just as a political platform does). A personal platform is what we stand for and what we stand on.[1]

A perspective also functions as a lens through which we look at the world of teaching. As a lens, a perspective affects our perception and interpretation of teaching. It does this by forming expectations of what we will experience (the *what* question), by helping us to understand basic reasons for the nature of the experience (the *why* question), and by offering standards for judging the quality of the experience (the *how well* question). Although some distortion is inevitable with any lens, without one we would see only what William James called "bloomin', buzzin' confusion." By becoming aware of the perspective by which we operate, we can at least become sensitive to the bases for our own approach to teaching, and, at best, become capable of changing our approach as we gain both new ideas and new teaching experiences. The primary goal of this chapter is to help you begin thinking about your own perspective on teaching; this thinking will make your perspective more explicit and thereby help to clarify it and reconsider its validity.

Where do perspectives come from? To be frank, the answer to this question has me puzzled. Clearly, past experience helps to shape perspectives. This chapter represents an attempt to help you understand the role of your past experiences in forming your present beliefs about teaching. Admittedly, I do not fully understand why some experiences have more impact than others or why different people experience the same set of events differently. But even without understanding the nature of human experience and its relation to perspectives, it is safe to claim that past experience is significant and that thinking about past experiences can contribute to the identification and examination of current perspectives on teaching.

The previous chapter examined the cooperating teacher's perspective on teaching. This chapter will be the first step in the initial formulation of your own perspective. There will be no "correct" answers to any of the exercises. Instead, they are intended to guide your thinking about your own approach to teaching, your own beliefs, ideals, commitments, principles, and values. In doing the exercises, you will examine two kinds of teaching-related experiences you have already had. First you have had extensive experience as a learner. Second, you have had some limited, mostly informal, experience as a teacher.

EXPERIENCE AS A LEARNER

> Those who cannot remember the past not only relive it; they tend to impose it, mistakes and all, on others.[2]

Not all learning is accompanied by teaching. In fact, some of our most potent learning experiences have taken place in the absence of any "teachers" (in both the formal and informal sense). There is no doubt, however, that much learning depends on effective teaching. We can examine our beliefs on learning and teaching by thinking about our own past experience as learners.

EXERCISE 6.1   Significant Learning Experiences

You might try to think about some potent learning experiences you have had. To do this, consider all experiences in which you learned something very significant, something which has stayed with you. A comprehensive list of settings is impossible, but let me try to help jog your memory. Consider the following contexts and people.

1. *Schools*—teachers in and out of classrooms, coaches, or extracurricular activities
2. *At home*—your parents, siblings, grandparents, and other relatives
3. *Chance meetings*—for example, people met while traveling
4. *Religious groups or events*—Sunday school, religious services, talks with religious leaders
5. *Workplaces*—bosses, fellow workers, customers
6. *Libraries*—school projects, pursuing a personal interest, or just plain browsing
7. *Music instruction*—classes, self-instruction, informal teachers
8. *Friendships*—peers, friends much older or much younger than you
9. *Counseling*—e.g., psychological, legal, or drug counselors

Spend five or ten minutes writing down the three most potent and significant learning experiences you can recall. Each experience should have had relatively discrete duration, that is, a time during which you were learning something important to you.

▶

When I have asked my own students to do this exercise, roughly one-third of them have mentioned one of their college teachers, one-fourth mentioned one of their elementary or secondary school teachers, one-fourth mentioned one of their family members, especially their mothers or fathers, one-fourth mentioned a nonschool music or sports teacher, and one-tenth mentioned a close friend. For many of my students, the significant learning experiences have no teacher. The conditions for a powerful learning experience are apparently set by such factors as the intensity of the situation, the person's own emotional state, and being on one's own. For example, many students mention their first year in college or the death of a friend, relative, or pet as powerful learning experiences.

What follows is the work of three students who were asked to do this exercise. Perhaps reading their work will help you to see what types of experiences qualify and how to describe them.

STUDENT RESPONSE 1

Taking a course in critical thinking and analytical writing during my first semester in college. The classroom setting was not crucial to the learning experience, and most of the learning was done by working on essays. The experience was special to me in that I felt I had created something unique, a product of my own thinking that no one could have constructed in the same way. At the time, I was eager to learn this subject and to learn if I could make it in college at all.

The sudden death of a close friend in my hometown. I learned how close death can really be and that no one loved should be taken for granted. The setting was crucial to the experience in that I attended the funeral and Mass and saw how others experienced it also. The learning was personal in that the person involved meant a lot to me. I needed to learn why I felt the way I did about his dying, searching for reasons for these feelings.

The setting was my home when I took up the hobby of silent motion picture collecting and reading. I absorbed a tremendous amount of information on the subject which, even 13 years later, comes easily to mind. At the time (1969) I was one year shy of draft eligibility and consciously interested in learning about other, better times.

STUDENT RESPONSE 2

The three most potent learning experiences were *learning sign language, learning how to be a better friend,* and *learning about my father's World War II experiences.*

I learned sign language in a classroom situation and from working with hearing-impaired students. This learning experience would be considered to be "subject matter." It is also a way of getting to know hearing-impaired people and helping them to get along better. I felt a strong need to learn so that I could communicate with the students on the only level they know how.

Learning how to be a better friend sounds vague and also like something that would take a lifetime. A very special friend gave me a crash course *just* by being my friend. She taught me a lot about myself. She taught me how to be a listener, how to be understanding and giving, and to be less selfish.

Learning about my father's WW II experiences was very important to me because not only did I learn about his life, I learned that he can be very open, given the opportunity. I learned from him while driving from Cornell to my home. I'll always cherish the experience because it was the first time in my life my father actually told me about something very emotional and important to him.

STUDENT RESPONSE 3

My first potent learning experience occurred when I was taking piano lessons from a blind man who was teaching me to play songs by ear. Usually, I would tell him that I wanted to learn a certain song I heard on the radio, and he would play it on the piano while taping what he was playing, I would take the tape home and learn the song. Finally, one day I asked him to teach me a certain song, and he told me to buy the single and learn it myself (without him as an intermediate step). I did this and was successful. I no longer needed his help to take what I was hearing (many different instruments) and play it on the piano. This was important because it set the stage for my future as a musician—playing by ear is sometimes very convenient. It also helped me to write my own music, indirectly.

Another experience was when I learned the quantum theory of the elements. I was having a difficult time grasping it and was feeling frustrated and stupid. A teacher of mine kept patiently explaining it to me, and when it finally became clear, I felt like shouting "Eureka!" through the halls of the school.

A third experience was when I learned to windsurf. This was important to me because I'm not very athletic, and I felt like I was broadening my horizons. I had a teacher who imparted the basic knowledge, but I learned mostly by practicing with this knowledge in mind (got very wet in the process!!). When I finally got the hang of it, I was very proud because others were trying it too— some not as successfully—and I sort of made it look easy!

Next, you might profit from analyzing your three learning experiences. For example, try to identify and write down why each was potent for you. You might warm up for this analysis by first trying it on the three sample responses you have just read. What elements made each experience significant? Consider the following:

- *Context.* In what setting did each experience occur? In a classroom or elsewhere? Was the setting crucial to the experience?

- *Teacher.* Who was involved? Were you alone or with others? Did a "teacher" bring about an experience, or did you, or did it happen spontaneously?

- *Subject matter.* Was there anything special about what you learned? Did the learning fall under the rubric of "subject matter," or was the learning more unusual and/or personal?

- *Learner.* Was there anything unique about *you* at the time of each experience? For example, did you feel an especially strong need to learn?

Next, try to draw generalizations about the conditions under which you learn best. Do you find any similarities or was each experience and learning process unique?

When I have asked undergraduate students to do this exercise, roughly half of the learning experiences have turned out to be instances of either learning without a teacher or learning with a nonschool teacher. Clearly students bring to our classrooms things they have learned outside classrooms as well as inside other classrooms. We all know this fact, but we all seem to forget it periodically.

On the basis of this exercise, consider your uniqueness as a learner and how this might affect your teaching. How have your past learning experiences affected your views on teaching? For example, as a consequence of your experiences, how important is it for teaching to involve the following:

1. A close relationship with the teacher
2. Being intrinsically motivated to learn
3. Learning nonacademic subject matter
4. Intense emotion surrounding the learning experience
5. A feeling of competence or success by the learner

If your past learning experiences have strongly affected your views, consider the validity of generalizing the conditions under which *you* learn best to conditions of learning for others. In particular, consider the limitations imposed by classroom teaching on providing the conditions required for your most significant learning experiences. Which of your conclusions are generalizable to most public school classroom teaching?

▶

Now we look more specifically at your past classroom teachers, since it is likely that they have contributed a great deal to your conceptions about teaching. It is experiences with past classroom teachers that constitute what Dan Lortie[3] describes as the 13,000-hour "apprenticeship by observation" that people experience before they even reach college.

EXERCISE 6.2   Most Successful and Unsuccessful Teachers

Try to think back over your 13 to 16 years of elementary, secondary, and higher education. Try to identify the two or three most unsuccessful teachers you can remember. Write their names, or some identifying characteristics if you cannot remember their names. Now jot down next to each what made that person so unforgettable. Do you think most of his or her other students would agree with you, or was your response to this teacher somewhat special? Was this teacher successful with any students? If so, what makes them different from you? What was the subject matter? Was this a factor in your response? Were there special circumstances with regard to community, the school, the class, the teacher's personal life, or your own state of mind? Would you find this teacher just as intolerable today?

▶

Now try to think of the two or three most successful teachers you have ever had. Jot their names down or write something down to identify each of them. What made each of them so successful? What did each of them teach? Was the subject matter a factor in each teacher's success? Do you think other students responded to these teachers as favorably as you? Who might disagree, and how are these students different from you? Were there any special circumstances such as a new and exciting curriculum or special events occurring in the school, community, or world (e.g., space shots, book censorships, a science fair)? Would you find each of these teachers just as wonderful today?

▶

Look over your two lists and notes. What did the teachers do that made them successful or unsuccessful? What can you conclude about teaching?

▶

If you have the opportunity, compare your conclusions with those of your present classmates. Discuss with them what makes your conclusions, and therefore your perspective on teaching, different from theirs. Consider the extent to which your school experiences have contributed to your views about teaching. To what extent have you examined these views? Often we operate from a set of assumptions that affect our expectations, judgments, and preferences of which we are not even aware. It is one thing to operate from a set of unexamined beliefs and another to hold onto those beliefs dogmatically in the face of contrary evidence. As long as we remain tentative about our beliefs and continually try to test them, we continue to grow.

EXERCISE 6.3   Student Belief Inventory

Many of the beliefs we hold as teachers are derived from our perspectives as students. In Chapter 8 you will respond to a set of statements designed to help you identify your perspective on your field experience as a teacher. In this exercise you will respond to a set of statements intended to elicit your perspective on being a student.

Note: 1 = Strongly disagree ("For the most part, no")
   2 = Disagree but with major qualifications ("No, but . . . ")
   3 = Agree but with major qualifications ("Yes, but . . . ")
   4 = Strongly agree ("For the most part, yes")

Control

1. My instructors should have complete control over each of the following:
1 2 3 4   a. teaching methods
1 2 3 4   b. classroom rules
1 2 3 4   c. selection of textbooks
1 2 3 4   d. curriculum and goals
1 2 3 4   e. administration of the school

2. Each of the following individuals or groups should have a say in educational decisions that affect each of my classes:
1 2 3 4   a. college administrators
1 2 3 4   b. the faculty member in charge
1 2 3 4   c. other faculty members
1 2 3 4   d. myself
1 2 3 4   e. my parents
1 2 3 4   f. state officials
1 2 3 4   g. students in each class

3. Each of the following individuals or groups should have a say in the courses I take:
1 2 3 4   a. faculty members
1 2 3 4   b. state officials
1 2 3 4   c. my parents
1 2 3 4   d. myself
1 2 3 4   e. college administrators

Diversity

4. As a student I want to be treated like all other students when it comes to each of the following:
1 2 3 4   a. methods
1 2 3 4   b. evaluation criteria
1 2 3 4   c. time offered to students
1 2 3 4   d. teacher's expectations for my achievement level

Learning and Motivation

1 2 3 4   5. I learn best when lessons are laid out as a series of carefully sequenced steps.

1 2 3 4   6. I learn best when left on my own to figure things out.

1 2 3 4   7. My motivation for learning derives more from intrinsic interest and curiosity than from external rewards.

Role of the Teacher

1 2 3 4   8. It is more important for me to respect than to like my instructors.

1 2 3 4   9. I prefer my instructors to be friendly and personal than to project a businesslike attitude.

School and Society

1 2 3 4   10. I don't think it proper for my instructors to let students know about their political preferences or their criticisms of the college administration.

1 2 3 4   11. Everything that I learn is related to every other thing.

1 2 3 4   12. All students (including myself) should have to study a core of studies that represent the basic elements of a good education.

1 2 3 4   13. My education should emphasize a broad background in the liberal arts, rather than specialized training.

It might be interesting to compare your responses on this Student Belief Inventory with those of your classmates. How do you account for differences and similarities? Another interesting comparison is your responses to the Student Belief Inventory versus your responses to the Teacher Belief Inventory in Chapter 8. In that chapter you will be able to reflect on the degree to which your perspective on teaching has been influenced by your student perspective and the appropriateness of one to the other.

EXPERIENCE AS A TEACHER

In Chapter 1 you made an inventory of your prior teaching experiences. Now you can examine them as sources of your initial perspective on teaching.

EXERCISE 6.4   Analysis of Prior Teaching Experiences

For each of the prior teaching experiences you listed in the exercise in Chapter 1, try to analyze the extent and the nature of your success. Remember, we are referring to nonformal teaching in addition to formal teaching. The following form may help you perform this analysis.

FORM 6.1. ANALYSIS OF PRIOR TEACHING EXPERIENCES

Description of Experience (from Form in Chapter 1)	Success Rating (1 = Failure) (5 = Success)	Criteria for Judging Success	Factors in Success or Failure
1.			
2.			
3.			
etc.			

If you performed this analysis, what can you conclude about teaching? On what sorts of success criteria do you typically rely? To what extent do these criteria reflect your views about what is important in teaching? To what extent do these criteria depend on the teaching situation? Are you likely to use these criteria in your field experience?

▶

How successful have you been at teaching? To what extent has your success motivated you to pursue a career in teaching?

▶

What factors have contributed to your successes or failures? How likely is it that these factors will affect your success or failure during your field experience?

▶

To what extent and in what ways have your prior teaching experiences affected your beliefs about and ideals for teaching.

▶

NOTES

1. Decker Walker, "A Naturalistic Model of Curriculum Development," in *Curriculum: An Introduction to the Field,* ed. James Gress (Berkeley, Calif.: McCutchan, 1978).
2. Eliot Wigginton, *The Foxfire Book* (Garden City, N.Y.: Anchor Books, 1972), p. 10.
3. Dan Lortie, *Schoolteacher* (Chicago: University of Chicago Press, 1975).

CHAPTER 7

How Do Foundational Studies Contribute to Your Perspective?

Many teacher educators believe that a person's perspective on teaching is formed by more than the experiences that the person has had as learner and teacher. They cite the importance of concepts and theories drawn from certain disciplines. After all, they claim, teaching implies helping a student learn things which, in turn, contributes to the achievement of broader educational aims. Appropriate aims are, at least in part, a *philosophical* issue, and the nature of learning is a *psychological* issue. In addition, teachers and students operate in one of our society's most significant institutions and therefore teachers must take into account the *sociology* of teaching. Awareness of these aspects of teaching leads teacher educators to consider philosophy, psychology, and sociology as three of the "foundations" of teaching. Other foundational studies include the history, economics, and politics of teaching.[1] Most preservice teacher education programs, therefore, require some coursework in at least two or three of these disciplines.

For foundational studies to be useful to field experiences, we must find ways of using foundational studies to help us think about and thereby enrich these experiences. One way that the foundations can do this is by supplying concepts for interpreting a particular field experience. For example, philosophy offers concepts like the scientific method, autonomy, and structure of knowledge; psychology offers concepts such as feedback, transfer, and intrinsic motivation; and sociology offers concepts such as role, bureaucracy, socialization, socioeconomic status, and subculture. If these concepts help us to understand what is going on in a school or in a classroom, then they may be considered useful for the analysis.

Another way to understand the contributions of the foundations is to view them as a source of questions and issues which any thoughtful teacher must address. For instance, philosophy, among other things, raises questions about the purposes to which teachers should give highest priority—transmission of our cultural heritage, citizenship, self-fulfillment, or vocational development; psychology, among other things, raises questions regarding the effectiveness of competition for improving motivation; and sociology raises questions about such things as the kinds of values, norms, and social definitions implicitly taught through the rules, procedures, and grading practices established by the school and the teacher.

This chapter is to help you use your foundational studies as bases for reflection about your field experiences. Although your perspective on teaching could embody a wide range of possible issues, the six issues we discuss encompass many (but not all) dimensions of most teachers' perspectives. We will examine each issue as a possible dimension of your perspective on teaching and in order to identify concepts you might find useful for thinking about it. We will also analyze some possible positions on the issue, in order to help you clarify your own position.

The issues we will examine are control, knowledge, learning and motivation, the teacher's role, pupil diversity, and the relation between school and society. You may recall that we used these same six issues to organize the teacher interview questions in Chapter 5 and again in Chapter 6 in the Student Belief Inventory.

These six issues can be expressed as questions which a teacher's pespective might address:

SIX BASIC ISSUES OF TEACHING

1. *Control.* Who should control what goes on in teaching, and what should be the range of their control?
2. *Diversity.* How unique are learners and how should one treat learners on the basis of their differences?
3. *Learning.* How do people learn in terms of both the process of learning and the motivation for it?
4. *Role.* How formal (versus personal) should teachers be in their relations with the learners?
5. *School and Society.* To what extent do the sources of and solutions to teachers' problems require structural changes in schools or society?
6. *Knowledge.* What is knowledge? Is knowledge a given set of facts, concepts, and generalizations to be transmitted, or is it more a per-

sonal or social construction developed by processes of reasoning and negotiation?

Taken as a whole, the six basic issues cover a broad range. We can see this scope by locating each issue on our earlier map of four common features (see Figure 1.1). The issues of student diversity and how students learn clearly center on the *learners*. The teacher's role is obviously an issue centering on the *teacher* and how he or she relates to the learners. School and society issues can be considered primarily *contextual* issues in teaching. Issues regarding the nature of knowledge reflect a dominant concern for conceptions of the *subject matter* we teach. Issues of control cover all four common features.

Control

- "A teacher who cannot control the class cannot teach."
- "The most important lesson to be learned is respect for authority."
- "In a democratic society, the teacher should make all decisions democratically."

Maybe one or more of these common sayings reflect your own viewpoint on control. When we talk about control in teaching, we are concerned with issues of *who* controls *whom* and in *what areas* they should exert their control. The "who" and "whom" refer to teachers, students, parents, administrators, textbook publishers, and state education personnel, among others. "What areas" refers to the particular domains in which the teachers, students, and others might exert control. Issues of control include the following:

1. Whether or not the teacher is merely a middleman between the administration or textbook writers and the learner
2. How strict the teacher should be
3. How extensive the teacher's control is (as compared with that of the students, parents, administrators, etc.) in determining the amount of *time* spent on activities, and the *rules* of conduct in the classroom (both the number and the kind of rules)
4. Who should select and design classroom activities, the standards used to evaluate performance, and the goals of instruction.
5. How closely teachers must adhere to the school's goals and policies

Let us see what light we can expect foundation courses to shed on such questions of control. In an attempt to answer these questions, we will examine sociologically the teacher's rules and the socialization process as a means of controlling students, and the curriculum as a means of controlling both teachers and students.

First let us take a quick look at schools through the eyes of a sociologist. To most sociologists the school and the classroom are social systems embedded within broader social systems, that is, the community, state, and nation. Within any social system there is bound to be conflict and, therefore, coercion.[2]

One conflict "exists between the bureaucratic authority of administrators, based on their position in a hierarchy of offices, and the professional authority of teachers, based on their training in a body of theory related to learning."[3] Another conflict derives from the compulsory nature of schooling "which captures students for a prolonged period." This coercive situation drives students to "form their own subcultures, as a means of coping with the pervasive and systematic demands of school authorities." These subcultures increase the level of conflict, since they typically do not support the educational goals of the school's faculty and staff.

But some sociologists, rather than emphasizing conflict, point out that any social system depends to some extent on a "consensus" of values and beliefs, if that social system is to function.[4] The school attempts to achieve consensus by socializing students, that is, by teaching self-control, discipline, and respect for authority. Of all the beliefs and values the schools try to instill, some consensus theorists consider the most significant to be the belief that achievement is the basis for the allocation of people to occupational slots in the society.[5] But, other more critical sociologists claim, schools reward students not only on the basis of their achievement, but also on the basis of their social class.[6] Diverse sociological ideas, stemming from these different sociological theories, provide different bases for thinking about questions of control.

Rules. Rules, for the sociologist, express norms of behavior. The methods of their enforcement are an expression of the sanctions the teacher chooses to employ. The enforcement of rules, then, is one means by which the teacher deals with the inevitable conflict arising within an autocratic form of governance.[7] Further, the rules teachers enforce reflect the type of socialization process which the school promotes.[8]

Questions about rules you might want to consider are as follows:

What rules do you plan to make explicit to your class?

Should rules be made cooperatively with the class or should they be made only by the teacher?

Do you think you will expect students to follow any rules which you do not plan to state explicitly?

What will be the scope of both your explicit and implicit rules? That is, what will they cover? Consider the following areas:

- Speaking order
- Movement within the classroom
- Movement outside the classroom
- Arrival time
- Seating posture
- Noise level
- Format and neatness of written work
- Dress
- Manners (student-teacher and student-student)

What sorts of sanctions do you think you might impose on students who break rules? What sorts of sanctions would you never impose?
▶

Socialization and the Hidden Curriculum. Rules are explicit expressions of norms of behavior, but they are also the least effective form of regulation. Sociologists point out that schools prefer to have students follow norms of behavior without coercion. To the extent that the students internalize the school's norms, the need for rules decreases. Students who control themselves require few rules. In a sense, explicit rules cover only those areas for which socialization has been incomplete or ineffective.

You might want to consider the sorts of assumptions you make concerning socialization. For example, consider the sorts of norms you will expect students to follow in the absence of explicit rules.
▶

Often we base our expectations about student behavior on our own past experience. These expectations can lead to many surprises, however, if we happen to teach in a school with a student population much different from the schools we attended. Since the home is the basis for most of the socialization process, the more you know about the community, the better prepared you will be in dealing with your students. (See Chapter 4 for some suggestions on how to learn about the community.)

Some educational sociologists consider the school's norms of behavior to be manifestations of what they call a "hidden curriculum."[9] They claim that the hidden curriculum is a powerful means of "social control." Included within the concept of a hidden curriculum are many outcomes that may result (and may even be expected to result) from the enforcement of both explicit and implicit rules. These potential outcomes may include docility, how to sit still for long periods under crowded conditions, a belief that effort, neatness, and promptness are more important than achievement, a belief that students get what they deserve in school, a belief that one's personality must be kept under constant control, a respect for authority, and many others. You will likely find some of these outcomes desirable, some undesirable, and some controversial. Actually, it depends on your own view of schools. Some people discover the hidden curriculum and exclaim, "Oh, my goodness!" while others proclaim, "Thank goodness!"

You might consider the kind of hidden curriculum you would like to discover in schools, the kind you suspect exists but hope does not exist, and what to do with a hidden curriculum when you find one.[10] Your preferred hidden curriculum is an expression of your preferred kinds of social control.

A closely related issue raised by sociologists concerns the hidden curricula of different socioeconomic (SES) groups. Not only may low-SES groups sometimes receive different official curricula, they may also receive different hidden curricula. Some sociologists examine the rules enforced by teachers in schools within different communities.[11] For example, they find that, in contrast to classrooms in high-SES communities, classrooms in low-SES communities restrict movement more within the class and outside the classroom (e.g., require bathroom passes), allow for less student decision making with regard to topics, allow less independent project work, require more busy work, and allow less student-to-student talk in the classroom.

Consider the ways in which the hidden curricula of low-SES classrooms might differ from that of high-SES classrooms. Contrast what low-SES students might learn with what high-SES students might learn as a consequence of the classroom norms. Would you as a teacher treat low-SES students differently from high-SES students? If not, what do you think accounts for the findings of sociologists? Maybe you are different from the teachers in the sociological studies just mentioned.

▶

The Curriculum as a Means of Control. Norms may be the most obvious means of control, but plans also control. One type of plan is the curriculum. Whether a curriculum is conceived as a plan describing intended instructional methods (i.e., means), intended learning outcomes (i.e., ends), or both, it controls both the teacher and the student by legitimizing some types of content and activities and delegitimizing others.

The more bureaucratically organized the school, the farther up the hierarchy important decisions are made. Yet the more teachers seek to professionalize their occupation, the more *they* want to make important decisions themselves. This conflict between teachers and administrators often centers on selection of textbooks, methods, and curriculum. Attempts to "standardize" the curriculum can be seen as attempts to further bureaucratize the school and, thus, to deprofessionalize teachers.

To what extent do you intend to follow the school's curriculum, if you happen to disagree with it? To what extent do you believe you should "adjust your teaching to the administration's view of good teaching practice" and be "obedient, respectful, and loyal to the principal" regarding matters of curriculum?[12]

▶

The school's curriculum defines what is to count as "school knowledge," as opposed to "non-school everyday knowledge."[13] For sociologists like Weber,[14] curricula are defined in terms of a dominant group's idea of the "educated person."

Some sociologists are concerned with how the imposition of certain knowledge (i.e., curricula) on lower SES groups prevents these groups from thinking for themselves.[15] These sociologists suggest that the dominant group's "common sense" becomes legitimized by being labeled "school knowledge" (and by being made available to certain groups through the official curriculum), while other groups' common sense is ignored.

This sociological perspective goes a step further to describe the sort of knowledge that is characterized as school knowledge and thereby is included in the school's curriculum. According to these sociologists, knowledge that serves "to legitimate a rigid hierarchy between teacher and taught"[16] is accorded the highest status. Such high-status knowledge is likely to manifest "a clear distinction between what is taken to count as knowledge, and what is not."[17] Furthermore, high-status knowledge is likely (1) to emphasize written rather than oral presentation, (2) to emphasize individual rather than group work in both instruction and evaluation, (3) to be abstract, and (4) to be "at odds with daily life and common experience."[18]

You might consider how you would characterize the subject matter you intend to teach according to this perspective:

1. Its status
2. The students to whom it will and will not be made available
3. The likelihood that different curricula in this subject matter will be offered to different students (e.g., different "tracks")

Philosophical and Psychological Perspectives on Control. This analysis of control-related issues is certainly not exhaustive. For example, the sociological discussion of the teacher's enforcement of rules could have included psychologically based techniques for "managing" classrooms, such as behavior-modification techniques. The predominantly sociological discussion of the teacher's responsibilities for the official curriculum of the state or school could have included philosophical analyses of liberty and academic freedom, including an analysis of who is entitled to control what and for whom.[19] The sociological discussion of knowledge could have included a philosophical analysis of the educated person. It could also have included a psychological analysis of the likely transfer-of-learning (i.e., "generativeness") that different subjects offer or a theoretical account of the relationship among knowledge, attitudes, and actions. These discussions only suggest the range of possible contributions to issues of control offered by philosophy, sociology, and psychology.

Learning and Motivation[20]

If you have ever taken an educational psychology course, there is likely to be no doubt in your mind that questions regarding learning and motivation are based on psychological theory. Whether they discuss learning or motivation, educational psychology courses often contrast behaviorist and cognitive theories. Behaviorist accounts of learning provide concepts such as the following to describe learning and teaching:

- *Law of exercise:* Repetition of a conditioned response strengthens the bond between the stimulus situation and the response; i.e., practice makes perfect
- *Reinforcement:* Anything that increases the strength of a behavior, with positive reinforcement using rewards and negative reinforcement using the withdrawal of unpleasant situations
- *Partial reinforcement:* Less than 100 percent reinforcement of responses
- *Operant conditioning:* Eliciting behaviors and then reinforcing them
- *Shaping:* Reinforcement of successive steps or approximations toward an ultimate target behavior
- *Modeling:* Providing a demonstration of a behavior for learners to observe and then to imitate
- *Self-pacing:* Pacing placed under learner control
- *Frame:* A step in a program which ends by having learners make an active response
- *Active responses:* A response requiring action (e.g., underlining the correct answer)

These concepts allow us to think about questions regarding teaching. For example, should we rely only on positive reinforcement? How small should our instructional steps be? How much modeling should we use in addition to verbal explanations?

Cognitive theories of learning introduce a different set of concepts. For example:

- *Insight:* Seeing all at once the solution to a problem (i.e., "Aha!")
- *Assimilation:* The incorporation of new ideas into an existing cognitive structure
- *Cognitive structure:* An interrelated set of concepts, beliefs, and information that a person has in his or her mind
- *Cognitive dissonance:* Discrepancy, incongruity, or gap between existing knowledge and a new learning task or experience
- *Spiral curriculum:* Successively returning to an idea at increasing levels of sophistication
- *Reception versus discovery learning:* Presentation of content to learners in final form versus allowing the learners to figure it out for themselves
- *Meaningful versus rote learning:* Content being related to the learner's cognitive structure in a nonarbitrary fashion versus the learner's acquiring information that he or she does not integrate into cognitive structure
- *Advance organizers:* Introductory material that acts as a cognitive framework for subsequent instruction
- *Short- versus long-term memory:* One aspect of information storage which is very limited in capacity versus another aspect of information storage which is virtually unlimited in capacity but from which retrieval is often difficult

These concepts allow us to raise further questions about learning: For example, how can we deepen the learners' insights into the meaning of the content we teach? What sorts of advance organizers will help people learn the new material meaningfully? How much cognitive dissonance is productive?

To make matters more complicated, behaviorists and cognitive learning theorists share certain terminology also, although they typically attach different meanings to each term and reach different conclusions. For example, behaviorists claim that errors should be minimized so as to avoid learning them, while cognitivists claim that people learn best from their errors.

Behaviorists and cognitive learning theorists also are in agreement on certain general principles, although they may explain them differently. Thus, they are both likely to claim that attention, modeling, and practice with feedback are likely to improve performance, but they will explain why in very different theoretical terms.

These basic differences would likely result in different views regarding some common teaching practices. For example:

1. *Setting up a laboratory experiment.* Behavioristic approach: the laboratory is for training learners in laboratory skills and scientific behaviors. Cognitive approach: the laboratory gives the learners an opportunity to make a discovery and to confront some evidence that challenges or conflicts with their existing ideas.
2. *Designing or selecting instructional material* (e.g., workbooks, texts, films). Behavioristic approach: instructional material should build complex skills out of simpler prerequisite skills, attempting to minimize learner errors by proceeding in small enough steps. Cognitive approach: instructional material should present the entire framework at the outset (perhaps by using an analogy or a good example) with the remainder of the material successively adding refinement, sophistication, and detail to the framework while allowing the students to learn from mistakes and to figure out some things for themselves through intelligent guessing.
3. *Giving tests.* Behavioristic approach: tests directly measure the attainment of the teacher's objectives, letting the teacher know whether the class has mastered the objective and giving the learner positive reinforcement, thereby increasing the strength of the behavior. Cognitive approach: tests offer highly indirect indicators of what is really going on inside a learner's head (e.g., conceptual development), allowing the teacher to analyze student misconceptions and errors, and giving the learners information they can use as a basis for modifying ideas and performance. The behaviorist believes that anything that has meaning can be observed and measured, while the cognitivist believes that many important things we learn are unobservable and therefore cannot be measured in any direct sense.

As expected, behaviorist and cognitive theorists also differ in their explanations of motivation.

Behavioral psychologists suggest that behavior is determined by past reinforcements and the contingencies in the present environment (i.e., a concern with incentives, habits), . . . and thus more concerned with observable behavior. Cognitive psychologists believe that people decide what they want to achieve, and that their thought processes control behavior . . . [Therefore, they] are most concerned with perceptions (e.g., discrepancies), information processing, understanding, and curiosity.[21]

Thus, while behavioral psychologists talk about *selecting* and *fixing responses* through *reinforcement* and *eliminating* or *extinguishing* others,[22] cognitive psychologists talk about how people perceive and think about themselves and about their success.

> Behaviorists place more emphasis upon external rewards and the deliberate and systematic arrangement of reinforcement contingencies, whereas cognitive theorists place more emphasis upon internal rewards and related cognitive processes.[23]

While behaviorists emphasize extrinsic motivation, cognitivists stress intrinsic motivation. Many cognitivists believe that curiosity is a natural and spontaneous characteristic of all people, especially children. Other, more eclectic educators believe that curiosity and intrinsic interest are unreliable sources of motivation for the majority of learners and that extrinsic rewards must be used initially to involve learners in productive tasks. Once involved, the tasks themselves will often supply intrinsic motivation. What is your view?

▶

Whether your view emphasizes extrinsic or intrinsic rewards, you probably have fairly strong beliefs about competition as a motivator. Maybe you agree with Johnson and Johnson:

> Competition is threatening and discouraging to those who believe they cannot win and many students will withdraw or only half-try in competitive situations. The whole area of intrinsic motivation shows that motivation does not depend upon competition. Even in extrinsic motivation situations, competition will exist only when there is a limited amount of the reinforcer which cannot be shared with everyone, and when everyone believes he has a chance of winning.[24]

If you agree with Johnson and Johnson, you will likely prefer cooperative classroom environments, not only for motivational purposes but also for the contribution of cooperative environments to social development.

Perhaps, however, you disagree with them and believe instead that competition is a fact of life and that, whether or not it heightens motivation, it is nevertheless an important lesson to be learned in schools in its own right.

Consider your own view of the role of competition and cooperation in the classroom. Think about your own classroom and whether it would emphasize a cooperative or competitive environment. Maybe your answer would vary with different learners.

Consider, for example, some common teaching practices from the perspective of your beliefs about motivation.

1. If you were marking student papers, consider whether you would let the entire class know who did the best, or whether individual success should be a private matter. Think about the emphasis of your comments on the papers, whether for reinforcement (e.g., praise), for challenging student responses and for raising further questions, or for both purposes.

▶

2. If you were organizing the classroom for a set of tasks (e.g., experiments, math problems, art projects, map work, etc.), consider whether you would want to organize students into groups or would prefer to have them work individually. Would you want students to cooperate on the work or to compete with each other? When choosing the problems or projects on which they work, how important would it be to you that students be initially interested in the work?

▶

Maybe a course in educational psychology has already challenged your beliefs on learning and motivation by presenting alternative views. Maybe such a challenge lies in front of you. Educational psychology has the potential to help you understand the psychological assumptions on which many of your beliefs rest, to help you reconsider those assumptions, and to give you a technical vocabulary to discuss issues of learning and motivation.

Diversity of Learners

TEACHER 1: It's only fair to treat all learners equally.

TEACHER 2: Yes, but we must respond to their individual needs.

STUDENT TEACHER: But which one of you is right?

In a one-on-one teaching situation, we typically respond to the learner as an individual. When we are faced with 30 learners, the complexity of the situation multiplies geometrically. How we view learners and how we treat them in group situations is crucial to our teaching. Whether we perceive each learner as unique or as a member of a category (e.g., slow, handicapped, poor, disruptive) and whether we treat learners equally regardless of their differences (or differently because of their differences) determines many of our teaching practices. For example, opinions differ regarding the teacher's allocation of time, based on special learner needs and regarding the individualization of objectives, content, pace, method of instruction, standards, and rules.

People disagree about special considerations for special learners partly because they disagree about what qualifies as a *special need*. Both sociology and psychology provide concepts to describe differences among learners; that is, these disciplines provide a variety of labels for categories of "specialness." Although particular schools and agencies have particular policies with regard to special needs, ultimately the teacher decides which of the characteristics are relevant to teaching practices (e.g., what to expect of learners, how much time to give them, and what rules they must follow).

Let us begin with a list of *general characteristics* drawn from psychology and sociology, which we can use to describe learners: I.Q., sex, socio-economic status, ethnicity, personality type, developmental stage, family lifestyle, attention span, and reading level.

Now also consider a list of *labels* for students drawn from these two disciplines:

gifted and talented	disadvantaged or culturally deprived
learning disabled	anxious
highly verbal	competitive
only child	hyperactive
concrete operational	creative
dogmatic	

Consider also a list, not necessarily drawn from psychology and sociology, but nevertheless part of the everyday language of educators:

"jock"	hard-working or lazy
over-or under-achiever	college bound or terminal
bright or slow	immature or serious

Of course, none of these lists is exhaustive. The point is that there are many possible ways to label and categorize learners.

Some sociologists, by studying particular schools and communities in depth, identify the different ways in which teachers and administrators treat different students, particularly those of differing socioeconomic statuses. These researchers note that, depending on how they categorize a student, teachers apply different rules, employ different sanctions when students break rules, have different academic and occupational expectations, apply different academic standards, seek different amounts of student input in instructional decision making, allocate different amounts of instructional time, and teach different content. Such practices may tend to limit students' opportunities for upward social mobility and might act as a set of self-fulfilling prophecies regarding the relationship between SES and achievement.

However, the point is not to claim that we should ignore all differences among learners, avoid individualization, and not tailor our teaching to the learners' needs. Treating learners as unique individuals is not the same as labeling and then treating them as members of groups. By categorizing learners, we might stereotype and obscure their individualities. More important, labeling and grouping learners, to some sociologists, runs the risk of limiting the educational opportunity of some students while maximizing it for others. That is, there is always the danger that, in our good intentions to meet their needs, we may be practicing a subtle form of discrimination.

Do you plan to group learners in your classroom? If so, on what basis? Would the different groups get different amounts of your time, or different materials? What undesirable short- or long-term consequences of this differential treatment should you be careful about?

▶

Whether or not you plan to group learners, your class is likely to be a heterogeneous mixture of learners. If you teach more than one class, the classes will differ in composition. How do you plan to deal with the diversity of learners? What is your attitude toward learners who come from backgrounds different from your own?

▶

Knowledge

The subject matter is typically taken for granted as the stable "stuff" of teaching, and yet it is the center of a very important set of issues affecting daily teaching practice. Traditionally, debates about knowledge in philosophy of education have concerned the nature of truth. Different philosophies propose different views of truth: truth as the coherence of ideas for idealists, truth as correspondence to reality for realists, truth as the product of reason and intuition of neo-Thomists, truth as what works for experimentalists, or truth as existential choice for existentialists.[25]

How do you view knowledge in your subject matter? Do you think of learning your subject matter as absorbing ideas (idealism), mastering facts and information (realism), training the intellect (neo-Thomism), problem solving (experimentalism), or finding the self (existentialism)?[26]

▶

More recently, philosophical debates about knowledge have concerned the way in which scientific ideas change and science progresses. Today's philosophers of science, such as Thomas Kuhn and Stephen Toulmin, reject the nineteenth-century "empiricist" view that science changes as a result of the accumulation of new facts and observations and the refinement of generalizations based on them. They also reject the empiricist requirement that scientists observe what is "really there" and be objective in their descriptions. In contrast, modern philosophy of science contends that science changes as a result of the failure of current theory to solve important scientific problems. Old theories are rejected and replaced by new ones, based on assumptions significantly different from those of the theories they are replacing. This "conceptual change" view argues further that our concepts and theories determine what we see. People with different theories can live in different perceptual worlds. Thus, what scientists see is affected by their scientific theories and concepts.[27]

These philosophical views have important implications for teaching practice. Consider, for example, three contrasting views on teaching as they relate to empiricist and conceptual change philosophies of science.[28]

A *didactic* view of teaching, primarily aimed at transmitting knowledge, relies on clear explanations, experiments, or demonstrations employed in support of the explanations, and guides discussions by using convergent questions, hints, and explanations. This view assumes learning to be the addition of new knowledge—a view consistent with empiricist ideas about the growth of knowledge.

A *discovery* view of teaching assumes that "students develop knowledge for themselves through active investigation and discovery."[29] The teacher focuses on student observations and measurements, acceptance of student responses to questions, and an absence of teacher presentations. This view is also fundamentally empiricist, particularly in its emphasis on objective observations "uncontaminated" by theories and in its claim that knowledge develops inductively from observations.

Both of these views have been criticized by the *interactionist* view,[30] a view based on a conceptual change philosophy. The *interactionist* view of teaching argues that students arrive in the classroom with well-formed, though often incorrect, ideas. Didactic teaching rejects or ignores these ideas. Discovery teaching allows students to develop further and refine their naive ideas through active experimentation, whether or not their naive ideas are true. In contrast with these two views, the *interactionist* view is more adversarial, recognizing the necessary interaction among students' naive ideas, their empirical observation, and the curriculum content. Such a view requires the teacher

> to bring out the students' preconceptions, provide a base of relevant experience and observations, challenge the students' misconceptions with appropriate questions and evidence, clearly present the . . . conception (to

be learned), and help the student to realize the greater power and usefulness of the new conception.[31]

Although these contrasting views refer primarily to science teaching,
how well do you think they relate to your own teaching? To what extent
will your students come with preconceptions that will conflict with what
you plan to teach?

▶

Obviously, discussions of knowledge are not independent of discussions of learning. After all, "to come to know" and "to learn" are two
different ways of expressing similar ideas. The distinction between the psychological term *learn* and the philosophical term *know* rests primarily on
the kinds of questions the two disciplines ask regarding knowledge and its
acquisition. While educational psychologists investigate the actual processes
through which people acquire knowledge, philosophers explore the nature,
limits, and validity of knowledge, rationality, and inquiry. Therefore, it
should not be surprising to find psychological theories that complement
philosophical views on knowledge. Simply (or simplistically) stated, behav-
iorism is a modern expression of traditional empiricism, and cognitive psychology (particularly the work of Piaget, Kohlberg, and modern informa-
tion-processing theorists such as Donald Norman) is consistent with a
"conceptual change" viewpoint.

Not only do philosophical orientations relate to psychological theories,
they also have sociological dimensions. We have already seen that knowledge to the sociologists may be considered a means of control (see pp. 75–
80). Berlak and Berlak point out additional sociological dimensions of
knowledge. They suggest that the traditional philosophical distinction between knowledge viewed as "given" (e.g., in realism) versus knowledge
viewed as "problematic" (e.g., in experimentalism) has significant sociological implications:

> Patterns that are predominantly *given* would, we suppose, convey un-
> questioning reverence and respect for the public knowledge transmitted
> by society through its agents, and ultimately for the society and its institu-
> tions as well, while heavily *problematic* patterns would convey a disposi-
> tion towards criticism and analysis, of culture and society, and encourage
> creativity.[32]

Further, they suggest that teachers may view knowledge differently for
different types of learners (see the issue of "diversity") and for different
subjects. If knowledge as given (e.g., emphasizing facts) underlies our
teaching of one racial, ethnic, or socioeconomic status group but not others

(e.g., emphasizing critical thinking), we may be implying that certain types of people should learn to criticize their culture and society and to be creative but other types of people should learn to accept and adjust to society's institutions. Berlak and Berlak[33] also point out that knowledge in some realms (e.g., mathematics and history) is treated as given and certain, while knowledge in other realms (e.g., literature) is treated as problematical. This differential treatment might well vary from school to school and from teacher to teacher.

In your view, is the knowledge in some subject matters more certain than in others? Should some kinds of students come to view your subject matter as certain while others develop a view of it as being less certain, more problematic? How do the tests and homework that teachers give and the way in which teachers administer and mark them convey a teacher's position on this issue?

▶

Role of the Teacher

"Be a real person." *(Carl Rogers)*
"Children don't want teachers to be their friends, they want someone to look up to." *(Common advice to new teachers)*

Many sociologists point out that schools are both agencies of socialization and bureaucratic organizations. In their attempts at socialization, they try to promote the kinds of learning and development they deem necessary for the growth of children into responsible, productive, and competent adults. For many educators this process requires warm interpersonal relations tailored to the uniqueness of each individual. However, as bureaucratic agencies, schools often provide impersonal and uniform treatment. Thus, sociologically speaking, there is a conflict of roles.

Will you as a teacher be formal and businesslike with your class, maintaining sufficient social distance from the learners, or will you try to be more informal and friendly? How much of a shift in roles must occur when you move from one side of the teacher's desk to the other?

▶

If you ask "experts" for their advice on these questions, you are likely to hear conflicting views. The answers seem to depend a great deal on whom you ask. For example, compare the sociologist Willard Waller with Carl Rogers. According to Waller:

Social distance is characteristic of the personal entanglements of teachers and students. It is a necessity where the subordination of one person to another is required, for distance makes possible that recession of feeling without which the authority of another is not tolerable. . . . Between adult and child is an irreducible social distance that seems at times an impassable gulf. The distance arises from the fact that the adult has absorbed the heritage of the group, and represents therefore in some sense the man plus the wisdom of all his ancestors, whereas the child is much more the natural and uncultivated man, and from the fact that the adult has found his place in the world and the child has not. . . . To the natural distance between adult and child is added a greater distance when the adult is a teacher and the child is a student, and this distance arises mainly from the fact that the teacher must give orders to the child; they cannot know each other, for we can never know a person at whom we only peer through institutional bars. Formality arises in the teacher–pupil relationship as a means of maintaining social distance, which in turn is a means to discipline. . . . Most important of the means whereby distance is maintained . . . is that classroom procedure which defers the situation in an impersonal manner and excludes possibilities of spontaneous human interaction. This is the dry, matter-of-fact, formal procedure of the classroom, which gives nothing and asks nothing of personality, but is always directed at the highly intellectualized matter to be studied.[34]

Consider the validity of this statement as a description of the reality of classroom teaching. Maybe you can infer Waller's attitude toward formal teaching: a necessary evil, a necessary good, or neutral. It might be interesting to consider how he would respond to this excerpt from Rogers.

What are these qualities, these attitudes, that facilitate learning? . . . Perhaps the most basic of these essential attitudes is realness or genuineness. When the facilitator is a real person, being what she is, entering into a relationship with the learner without presenting a front or a facade, she is much more likely to be effective. This means that the feelings that she is experiencing are available to her, available to her awareness, that she is able to live these feelings, be them, and able to communicate them if appropriate. It means that she comes into a direct personal encounter with the learner, meeting her on a person-to-person basis. It means that she is *being* herself, not denying herself. . . . Thus, she is a person to her students, not a faceless embodiment of a curricular requirement nor a sterile tube through which knowledge is passed from one generation to the next. . . . It is obvious that this attitudinal set, found to be effective in psychotherapy, is sharply in contrast with the tendency of most teachers to show themselves to their pupils simply as roles. It is quite customary for teachers rather consciously to put on the mask, the role, the facade of being a teacher and to wear this facade all day removing it only when they have left the school at night.[35]

Rogers's current view is consistent with many "open education" writers around 1970 in the United States, like Charles Silberman:

Informal education relieves the teacher of the terrible burden of omniscience. . . . To the formal teacher, admitting ignorance means loss of dignity . . . In an informal classroom, by contrast, the teacher is the facilitator [note the term *facilitator* in both Rogers's and Silberman's writing] rather than the source of learning, the source being the child himself. . . . The consequence is an atmosphere in which everyone is learning together. . . . Most important, however, the free day classroom relieves the teacher of the necessity of being a timekeeper, traffic cop, and disciplinarian. In a formal classroom, a large proportion of the teacher's time and an extraordinary amount of energy are consumed simply by the need to maintain order and control. ("I cannot begin until all talking is stopped and every eye is on me!") In the informal classroom, the discipline problem withers away, in part because children are not required to sit still and be silent. . . . A[n] [informal] teacher with forty years' experience remarks, "I try to be informal. I mean, I try to make this situation as much as possible like a family group sitting around a fireplace or around a table when some question has come up and they're discussing it."[36]

Consider your own view of the Rogers/Silberman position. Are they being realistic? Perhaps the conflict between Waller's sociological and Rogers's psychotherapeutic analysis stems from a difference between a description of the ways things are and a proposal for the way things ought to be. Maybe different disciplines of knowledge (here, sociology and psychotherapy) offer different, even conflicting, perspectives on classroom teaching.
▶

More important, what is your view regarding the informal/formal issue? How informal or formal do you plan to be, and how do you plan to express your preferred role? Think about your role in terms of the sorts of clothing you plan to wear, how you will expect your students to address you, the rules for determining speaking order in the classroom (e.g., hand-raising), where and how you will position yourself in the classroom, how strict you will be, what you will do when one of your students tries to approach you on a personal matter (either yours or the student's), and what sort of differences there are between your in-class and out-of-class voice. Waller points out that these aspects of a teacher's behavior all affect the teacher's prestige.
▶

School and Society

"Teaching is subversive activity." (*Neil Postman and Charles Weingartner*)
"Dare the school build a new social order?" (*George S. Counts*)

"Schools merely reproduce the social order and perpetuate its class strati-
fications." *(various neo-Marxists)*
"Don't make waves!" *(Anon.)*

Perhaps one or more of these quotations reflect your view of teaching.

Of course schools are for learning. They are the society's primary
means for transmitting the cultural heritage from one generation to the
next. But some sociologists notice "two other fundamental and inseparable
purposes: (1) they keep lower-class students from competing equally with
middle-class students, and (2) they serve to legitimate the political and social
system."[37] Some sociologists view schooling as a "competitive struggle for
social and economic rewards. It is essentially a tug-of-war between the middle and lower classes, with the upper classes literally above the battle."[38]

But what roles do teachers play in this process? Although our personal
political posture does not necessarily influence our daily teaching practices,
most of us nevertheless have rather deep political convictions. These convictions may affect the teaching of social studies more than the teaching of
math, but it is difficult to escape the effect altogether in any teaching situation. "Either a teaching activity serves to integrate children into the current
social order, or it provides children with the knowledge, attitudes or skills
to deal critically and creatively with that reality in order to improve it."[39]
The contexts of our teaching can never be ignored for long.

Since the teacher is the primary political socializing agent for the child,
the teacher's political posture is crucial.

The teacher represents *the* authoritative spokesman of society, for the
teacher is usually the first model of political authority the beginning student encounters.[40]

With teachers playing such a crucial role in the socialization of
learners, some sociologists see the political orientation of teachers as a key
factor affecting the process of education:

The conservatism apparent in teachers is best understood, perhaps, by
considering them as advocates of the interests of the middle class. Teachers prefer to do regular rather than radical things, and they do not encourage their students to participate in politics other than in the most accepted
and established fashions. This interpretation is based upon the assumption that teachers charged with the responsibilities of injecting system
maintenance values into the educational subculture encourage their students to become good citizens, and in so doing, do not offer students an
alternative to acceptance of the *status quo.*[41]

These sociological claims regarding the purposes of schooling and the
socialization of students and teachers may strike you as obvious or as ab-

surd. Even if you accept these claims as valid, you may either applaud or deplore schools and teachers that serve these functions.

How do you see yourself in relation to the school and society? How politically conservative are you? How comfortable are you with people of more radical political persuasion? To what extent do you believe that the school is the *cause* of social inequalities? How supportive of "middle-class" values are you? For example, to what extent do you agree with each of the following middle-class beliefs:

1. A person's career is the most important determinant of status in our society.
2. My children should have the same educational opportunities as I have had.
3. A "good" school is one that is academically oriented.
4. Education is the pathway to economic achievement.

▶

Another way to assess your own political posture as a teacher is to consider classroom problems: Are the problems you face as a teacher basically educational problems solvable through educational means? Or do most of the problems require structural changes in schools and society? Clearly an affirmative answer to this last question reflects a less conservative view. Although the terms "conservative" and "progressive" have recently acquired many new and misleading connotations, they still denote two ends of a continuum that describes these basic issues.

From a philosophical point of view, this issue could be treated as a debate between reconstructionists and conservatives, between philosophers like Theodore Brameld and William Bagley:

> [*Brameld*]While repudiating nothing of the constructive achievements of other educational theories, reconstructionism commits itself, first of all, to the renascence of modern culture. It is infused with a profound conviction that we are in the midst of a revolutionary period out of which should emerge nothing less than the control of the industrial system, of public services, and of cultural and natural resources by and for the common people who, throughout the ages, have struggled for a life of security, decency, and peace for themselves and their children.[42]

> [Bagley] The very time to avoid chaos in the schools is when something akin to chaos characterizes the social environment. . . . The very time to emphasize in the schools the values that are relatively certain and stable is when the social environment is full of uncertainty and when standards are crumbling. Education follows, it does not lead. If education is to be a stabilizing force it means that the school must discharge what is in effect a disciplinary function. The materials of instruction, the methods of teaching, and the life of the school as a social organization must exem-

plify *and idealize* consideration, cooperation, cheerfulness, fidelity to duty and to trust, courage and perseverance in the face of disappointment, aggressive effort toward doing the task that one's hand finds to do and doing it as well as one can, loyalty to friend and family and those for whom one is responsible, a sense of fact and a willingness to face facts, clear and honest thinking. These may not be eternal values, but one may venture a fairly confident prediction that they will be just as significant a thousand years from now as they have ever been in the past.[43]

You might examine whether we are "in the midst of a revolutionary period," how "stable" our values are, and whether education follows or leads the society. What is your position regarding the reconstructionist-conservative debate, and how would your position affect your conduct as a teacher?

▶

INTERRELATIONS AMONG THE SIX ISSUES

As with most things in education, these six issues are highly interrelated. Beliefs about learning and motivation relate directly to beliefs about knowledge, the teacher's role, and control. For example, a person with a belief in cooperative learning environments *(learning)* might be likely to value a close relationship with pupils *(teacher role),* to base context decisions on the children's interests *(knowledge* and *motivation),* and to let the children participate fully in setting rules for classroom operations *(control).* Such a teacher might be labeled "informal." In contrast with this teacher is one who emphasizes grades (extrinsic *motivation*) and, perhaps, competition *(learning),* teaches mostly facts without worrying too much about how they relate to children's past experience *(knowledge),* sets rules of conduct and enforces them strictly but fairly *(control)* in a businesslike manner *(teacher role).* This teacher might be labeled "formal."

Labels such as formal/informal, traditional/progressive, and authoritarian/democratic might work well for extremes in teacher perspectives, but the vast majority of teachers' perspectives are too complex for such oversimplifications. Although our beliefs on one issue relate to our beliefs on another, the relationship is not entirely predictable. For example, a teacher who tries to develop a "good group" might have a self-image of a strong group leader, even as a benevolent dictator.[44] This emphasis on the group can lead to the teacher's exerting strong control of classroom behavior, being particularly strict with "uncooperative" behaviors. We shall return to a discussion of apparent inconsistencies in teacher beliefs in Chapter 10.

Each of the six issues is far too general for us to resolve in any definitive manner. The questions used to present them can be answered similarly: "It all depends!" Actually it all depends on the four common features we discussed earlier. It all depends on who the *teacher* is, who the *learners* are, what the *subject matter* is, and in what grade level, type of school, and community (i.e., *context*) the teaching is situated. Let us examine an example of the way the resolution of basic issues depends on what the subject matter is, who the learners are, what the context is, and who the teacher is.

Mrs. Borden[45] has definite views about *subject matter,* but her views differ for each subject. She monitors the morning's work in the *3Rs* much more closely than she does the afternoon activities—arts and crafts, music, and dramatic play. For the *3Rs* she keeps careful records of both time spent and accomplishments. She treats the arts, creative play, and social development more as rewards for work in the basics than as significant subjects in their own right. Social studies and science are learned through project work in which the pupils are allowed to choose their topics.

When we look at the differential treatment of *learners* in addition to subject matter, Mrs. Borden's resolution of the issues becomes striking, particularly with regard to the consequences of her practices for her pupils. Her "slower" pupils are those who cannot quickly memorize written words and/or have not acquired decoding skills. These pupils receive more step-by-step, less broad, more extrinsically motivated, less personally relevant instruction. For example, they spend more time memorizing words out of context and more time reading from books that control vocabulary in terms of structurally similar words (e.g., *hat, cat, mat,* etc.). Perhaps because these stories lack any interest value (and, therefore, intrinsic motivation), these "slower" children are constantly pushed to "get on with it." Because some of these children come from backgrounds somewhat different from those of the other children, the content of all the instruction is less likely to relate to the life they experience after school hours and beyond the school's walls.

As the *context* of the teaching shifts, so too will the teacher's resolution of the issues. As these "slower" children move up in grade level, they may spend more time being "remediated," receiving more extrinsic motivation and less meaningful and interesting content from their remedial reading *teacher,* who may increasingly treat them as clients. Meanwhile, their "regular" teachers are likely to exert far greater control over their "faster" classmates. Many aspects of this differential treatment could be accentuated if these pupils are from low-SES neighborhoods and if the teacher is middleclass and unfamiliar with low-SES people.

SUMMARY

Notice the terrain we have traveled in this chapter. Our discussion of *control* centered on a sociological analysis of rules, socialization, and the curriculum. However, at the end of this section we mentioned psychological and philosophical dimensions of control. We discussed behavioral and cognitive psychological dimensions of *learning and motivation.* We viewed the *diversity of learners* from a predominantly sociological perspective, on labeling and grouping people, though the labels themselves derive from both sociology and psychology. Whether knowledge is certain or problematic was the focus of our philosophical treatment of the *knowledge* issue, though we also analyzed knowledge as a sociological issue. When we discussed the *role of the teacher,* we compared one sociological view of social distance with one psychological view of genuineness. Our discussion of *school and society* included the socialization of teachers and students and a comparison between two philosophies, reconstructionism and conservatism.

Obviously each of the six issues serves as a focal point for a divergent set of foundational perspectives. The foundations of education help us raise questions and supply concepts for thinking about our own teaching practices. But the foundations cannot answer these questions. Answers reflect our own personal perspective on teaching which, in turn, depend on the situation in which we teach. In order to answer these questions, we must make a commitment to a view on what good teaching is and on what a good teacher does in a particular situation.

NOTES

1. Because of limited space, this book discusses only three of the disciplines: philosophy, psychology, and sociology.
2. Willard Waller, *The Sociology of Teaching* (New York: Wiley, 1932).
3. Robert Arnove, "On Sociological Perspective and Educational Problems," in *Education and American Culture,* ed. Elizabeth Steiner, Robert Arnove, and B. Edward McClellan (New York: Macmillan, 1980), p. 6.
4. Emile Durkheim, *Education and Sociology,* trans. Sherwood Fox (Glencoe, Ill.: Free Press, 1956).
5. Talcott Parsons, "The School Class as a Social System," *Harvard Educational Review* 29, Fall 1959.
6. Samuel Bowles and Herbert Gintis, *Schooling in Capitalist America: Educational Reform and the Contradictions of Economnic Life* (New York: Basic Books, 1976).
7. Waller, op. cit.
8. Parsons, op. cit.
9. Philip Jackson, *Life in Classrooms* (New York: Holt, Rinehart and Winston, 1968).
10. I borrowed this last point from Jane Martin, "What Should We Do with a Hidden Curriculum When We Find One?" in *The Hidden Curriculum and Moral Education,* ed. Henry Giroux and David Purpel (Berkeley, Calif.: McCutchan, 1983).

11. Jean Anyon, "Social Class and the Hidden Curriculum of Work," in *Curriculum and Instruction,* ed. Henry Giroux, Anthony Penna, and William Pinar (Berkeley, Calif.: McCutchan, 1981).

12. Ronald Corwin, *Militant Professionalism: A Study of Organizational Conflict in High Schools* (New York: Appleton, 1970), p. 234.

13. Basil Bernstein, "On the Classification and Framing of Educational Knowledge," in *Knowledge and Control: New Directions for the Sociology of Knowledge,* ed. Michael Young (London: Collier-Macmillan, 1971).

14. Max Weber, *Essays in Sociology,* trans. and ed. H. Gerth and C. W. Mills, (London: Routledge and Kegan Paul, 1952).

15. A. Gramsci, *The Modern Prince and Other Writings* (translation) (New York: Monthly Review Press 1957).

16. Michael Young, ed., *Knowledge and Control: New Directions for the Sociology of Education* (London: Collier-Macmillan, 1971), p. 36.

17. Ibid.

18. Ibid., p. 38.

19. See, for example, Kenneth Strike, *Liberty and Learning* (Oxford, England: Martin Robertson, 1982).

20. Much of this section is adapted from Thomas Good and Jere Brophy, *Educational Psychology: A Realistic Approach,* 2nd ed. (New York: Holt, Rinehart and Winston, 1980).

21. Ibid., pp. 210–211.

22. Ibid.

23. Ibid., p. 212.

24. David Johnson and Roger Johnson, "Instructional Goal Structure: Cooperative, Competitive or Individualistic," *Review of Educational Research* 44(2) (1974), 218.

25. Van Cleve Morris, *Philosophy and the American School* (Boston: Houghton Mifflin, 1961).

26. Ibid.

27. See Kenneth Strike and George Posner, "Epistemological Perspectives on Conceptions of Curriculum Organization and Learning," in *Review of Research in Education,* ed. Lee Shulman, Vol. 4 (Itasca, Ill.: F. E. Peacock, 1976); Harold Brown, *Perception, Theory and Commitment: The New Philosophy of Science* (Chicago: University of Chicago Press, 1977).

28. This discussion is based on Edward Smith and Charles Anderson, "The Effects of Teacher's Guides on Teacher Planning and Classroom Instruction in Activity-Based Science." Paper presented at the Annual Meeting of the American Educational Research Association, Montreal, April 1983.

29. Ibid., p. 19.

30. Smith and Anderson (ibid.) refer to this view as the "conceptual change" view.

31. Ibid., p. 19.

32. Ann Berlak and Harold Berlak, *Dilemmas of Schooling: Teaching and Social Change* (New York: Methuen, 1981), p. 148.

33. Ibid.

34. Willard Waller, *The Sociology of Teaching* (New York: Wiley, 1932), pp. 279–280.

35. Carl Rogers, *Freedom to Learn for the 80's* (Columbus, Ohio: Charles E. Merrill, 1983), pp. 121–122.
36. Charles Silberman, *Crisis in the Classroom: The Remaking of American Education* (New York: Random House, 1970), pp. 267–271.
37. Joseph Scimecca, *Education and Society* (New York: Holt, Rinehart and Winston, 1980), p. 24.
38. Ibid., p. 24.
39. Carl Grant and Kenneth Zeichner, "On Becoming a Reflective Teacher," in *Preparing for Reflective Teaching,* ed. Carl A. Grant (Boston: Allyn and Bacon, 1984), p. 15.
40. Scimecca, op. cit., p. 105.
41. Harmon Zeigler, *The Political Life of American Teachers* (Englewood Cliffs, N.J.: Prentice-Hall, 1967), pp. 21–22.
42. Theodore Brameld, adapted from *Education for the Emerging Age* (New York: Harper and Brothers, 1969), pp. 26–27.
43. William Bagley, *Education and Emergent Man* (New York: Ronald Press Co., 1934), pp. 154–156.
44. See Valeria Janesick, "An Ethnographic Study of a Teacher's Classroom Perspective." Unpublished Doctoral dissertation, Michigan State University, 1977.
45. A fictitious teacher inspired by several teachers described in Berlak and Berlak, op. cit.

ELON COLLEGE LIBRARY

CHAPTER 8

What Is Your Initial Perspective?

A thoughtful man is neither the prisoner of his environment nor the victim of his biography[1]

It always seems difficult to take a stand, to make a commitment. Maybe that is why people try to avoid taking a position on basic issues. But when you devote the time and energy and take the risks involved in formulating your views, you lay the groundwork for personal and professional growth. By making your perspective on teaching explicit, you can become a more reflective teacher, less likely to be a slave to your unexamined assumptions and more open to change based on your daily experiences.

In previous chapters you analyzed the situation in which you will teach and examined your past experiences and foundational studies as sources for a perspective on teaching. This chapter helps you to sort out your ideas about teaching and to come to terms with your current perspective.

SORTING OUT IDEAS

In Chapters 4 and 5 you analyzed the community, the school, the class-room, and the students. You also examined the cooperating teacher's per-spective. Perhaps you found yourself agreeing with the cooperating teacher. But maybe you would do things differently if you were in charge. An important part of your growth as a teacher will result from your examination of your beliefs about teaching.

One way to sort out ideas is to react to a set of assertions about teaching. Your reactions will help you examine your beliefs on teaching. These beliefs, taken as a whole, constitute your initial perspective.

EXERCISE 8.1   The Teacher Belief Inventory[2]

What if in your field experience you were fully responsible for the learners? Would you be the same teacher as the cooperating teacher or your co-worker(s) (if any), or would you differ in significant ways?

This exercise is designed to help you sort out your beliefs. In order to do it, you must decide the extent to which you, as the teacher in charge, agree or disagree with each of the following assertions. If you are not actually the teacher in charge in your field experience, respond *as if you were in charge*. Circle one response for each assertion. Respond only to those assertions that apply to your field experience. You will note that the assertions are grouped under headings corresponding to the six basic issues presented in Chapter 7.

Note: 1 = Strongly disagree ("For the most part, no")
      2 = Disagree but with major qualifications ("No, but. . . . ")
      3 = Agree but with major qualifications ("Yes, but. . . . ")
      4 = Strongly agree ("For the most part, yes")

Control

1 2 3 4   1. I would encourage parents to work with me inside the classroom.

1 2 3 4   2. Parents would have no right to tell me as a teacher what to do in the classroom.

1 2 3 4   3. As a teacher I should be left free to determine the methods of instruction that I use in the classrooms.

1 2 3 4   4. Parents would have the right to visit my classroom at any time if they gave me prior notice.

1 2 3 4   5. I would consider the revision of my teaching methods if these were criticized by the learners.

1 2 3 4   6. As a teacher I would rely heavily on the textbook and prepackaged materials, rather than trying to write and design my own.

1 2 3 4   7. Learners should have some control over the order in which they complete classroom assignments.

1 2 3 4   8. Learners should have some choice in the selection of classroom assignments.

1 2 3 4   9. I would feel free to depart from the official adopted curriculum when it seemed appropriate to do so.

1 2 3 4   10. Parents and other community members should have the right to reject school books and materials.

1 2 3 4   11. The principal or my department chairman should ultimately determine what and how I should teach.

1 2 3 4   12. What I teach will probably be heavily influenced by statewide or districtwide standardized tests.

1 2 3 4   13. As a teacher my primary task would be to carry out the educational goals and curricular decisions that have been formulated by others.

1 2 3 4   14. I would give learners some options for deciding *what* to study.

1 2 3 4   15. Parents should be active in formulating curriculum.

1 2 3 4   16. Parents should be involved in hiring teachers for their children's school.

1 2 3 4   17. I would be involved in administrative decisions in my school or organization (e.g., allocating the school's budget, hiring staff).

1 2 3 4   18. I would disobey official regulations when I felt that they interfered with the welfare of the learners.

1 2 3 4   19. I would allow learners to go to the bathroom at just about any time.

1 2 3 4   20. It is more important for learners to learn to obey rules than to make their own decisions.

1 2 3 4   21. I would encourage learners to speak spontaneously without necessarily raising their hands.

Diversity

1 2 3 4   22. I would employ multiple and diverse criteria to evaluate learners. It is not fair to use the same criteria to evaluate all learners.

1 2 3 4   23. If I taught classes that differed with regard to learners' academic ability, I would teach them differently.

1 2 3 4   24. I would not expect learners from economically disadvantaged backgrounds to assume the same degree of responsibility for their learning as learners from more economically advantaged backgrounds.

1 2 3 4   25. One of the main problems in classrooms today is diversity among pupils.

1 2 3 4   26. There should be set standards for each grade level and subject, and as a teacher I would evaluate all learners according to these standards.

1 2 3 4   27. I could probably do most for learners who want to learn.

1 2 3 4   28. I would attempt to devote more of my time to the least capable learners in order to provide an equal education for all.

1 2 3 4   29. I would lower my expectations regarding academic performance for those learners who come from economically disadvantaged backgrounds.

Learning

1 2 3 4   30. One of the most important tasks I would face as a teacher is developing individuals into a good working group.

1 2 3 4   31. I would use the comparison of one learner's work with that of another as a method of motivation.

1 2 3 4   32. People learn better when cooperating than when competing with one another.

1 2 3 4   33. I would lead learners through a series of easily mastered steps in such a way that the learners make as few errors as possible.

1 2 3 4   34. I would tell my students exactly what was expected of them in terms of behavior, homework, and lesson objectives.

1 2 3 4   35. Since people learn a great deal from their mistakes, I would allow learners to learn by trial and error.

1 2 3 4   36. I would use grades to motivate learning.

1 2 3 4   37. The sheer interest in learning something new and challenging or of successfully accomplishing a task usually supplies sufficient motivation for learning.

1 2 3 4   38. I would start out as a strict disciplinarian and gradually become more approachable as the learners come to respect my authority.

1 2 3 4   39. As a teacher I would tell learners a great deal about myself.

1 2 3 4   40. I would serve more as a group facilitator than as a transmitter of information.

School and Society

1 2 3 4   41. My political beliefs have no place in my teaching.

1 2 3 4   42. Schools and youth groups should seek to help all learners to fit as smoothly as possible into our present society.

1 2 3 4   43. I would not participate in local political activities when it involved criticism of local school authorities.

1 2 3 4   44. As a teacher I would be concerned with changing society.

1 2 3 4   45. There is a great deal that is wrong with the public schools today, and one of my priorities as a teacher would be to contribute as much as possible to the reform of public schooling.

1 2 3 4   46. The home backgrounds of many learners are the major reasons why those children do not succeed in school.

1 2 3 4   47. Schooling as it now exists helps perpetuate social and economic inequalities in our society.

1 2 3 4   48. It is as important for learners to enjoy learning as it is for them to acquire specific skills.

1 2 3 4   49. In the elementary grades, instruction in the *3 Rs* should take up most of the school day. Other subject areas (e.g., science, social studies) should be given less emphasis in the curriculum.

1 2 3 4   50. Students in high school don't spend enough time on the "basic" subjects.

1 2 3 4   51. Most high school courses try to cover too much material, thereby sacrificing real understanding.

1 2 3 4   52. My subject matter is more a body of content than it is a set of skills to be mastered.

1 2 3 4   53. One of the primary purposes of teaching my subject matter is to develop good work and study habits.

1 2 3 4   54. Schools today pay too much attention to the social-emotional needs of children, and not enough emphasis is given to academic skill development.

1 2 3 4   55. I would emphasize teaching the *3 Rs* more than the skills of problem solving.

1 2 3 4   56. It would be important to me to divide the school day into clearly designated times for different subject areas.

1 2 3 4   57. I would teach the knowledge of different subject areas separately, because important knowledge is overlooked when subjects are integrated.

ANALYSIS OF BELIEFS

Each basic issue encompasses 3 to 21 items. For further study select two or three basic issues or specific aspects of basic issues. It is probably more useful to focus on a small set of issues in depth than to attempt to think through your views on a wide range of issues. In order to make this selection, you might examine your responses to each item.

Which groups of items (i.e., issues) were most relevant to your field experience and, therefore, elicited some response?
▶

To which groups of items or issues were your responses most extreme (i.e., a response of 1 or 4)?
▶

To which groups of items or issues did you give a qualified response (i.e., a response of 2 or 3)?

▶

Which issues really concern you most?

▶

With this analysis of your responses in mind, you can decide now on which two or three issues you would like to focus your inquiry and explain the reasons behind your choice.

▶

Now you can examine your response to the groups of items you just selected and summarize and elaborate your responses to form a coherent answer to a selected subset of the following questions:

1. Control
   a. How should classroom procedures be determined? (Items 1–5)
   b. How should curriculum and content be determined? (Items 6–15)
   c. How much input should the teachers and parents have regarding the administration of the school? (Items 16–18)
   d. How much control should teachers have over learners' behavior? (Items 19–21)

▶

2. Diversity
   a. How should learners' differences be handled? (Items 22–29)

▶

3. Learning
   a. Is learning facilitated by an individualistic, competitive or cooperative environment? (Items 30–32)
   b. How does one acquire competence in a subject matter? (Items 33–35)
   c. What is the basis for motivation? (Items 36–37)

▶

4. Teacher's role
   a. How formal a role should the teacher assume? (Items 38–40)

▶

5. School and society
   a. How active should the teacher become in reforming the school and the society? (Items 41–45)
   b. Are schools the cause of social inequalities or are school problems merely the effects of these societal problems? (Items 46–47)

▶

6. Knowledge
   a. What should be the curriculum's emphasis? (Items 48–56)
   b. Should different subject matters be kept separate or integrated? (Items 57–58)

▶

For the purpose of future discussions, your responses to the Teacher Belief Inventory, together with your summary and elaboration of those responses focusing on two or three issues, constitute what we shall call your "initial perspective on teaching." This perspective is not a general philosophy of teaching but a set of beliefs regarding your specific field experience.

EVALUATING YOUR INITIAL PERSPECTIVE

At this point you can evaluate your initial perspective. This section contains some suggestions.

1. *The Community.* Refer to the situation analyses you did in Chapters 4 and 5. Begin by rereading your descriptions of the community and the neighborhood. Consider your perspective within the context of this setting, particularly your beliefs about the scope of parental control, learner diversity, the extent of control of learner behavior, the formality of the teacher's role, teacher activism in social reform, the school's relation to social problems, and curriculum emphasis. In the space provided, suggest areas of possible conflict between your perspective and the community expectations.

▶

2. *The School.* Now reread your conclusions about the school and its inhabitants (p. 42–46). Consider your perspective in the context of these conclusions. Will it be difficult for you to implement your perspective given what you know about the principal?

▶

Given what you know about the school's faculty?

▶

Given what you know about the school?

▶

3. *The Parents.* Reread your summary of the parental role in the learner's education. Consider your beliefs about appropriate parental control in the context of this finding. Any revisions?

▶

4. *The Learners.* Reread your summary of the learners' backgrounds and attitudes about people who are "different." Consider your beliefs about learner diversity in the context of their backgrounds and attitudes. Any revisions? Where might it be difficult to implement your perspective? Any areas of potential conflict?

▶

Reread your summary of the learners' ideal teacher. Consider your beliefs about the teacher's role in the context of their views. Any revisions?

▶

Reread your summary of the learners' goals and aspirations. Consider your beliefs about curriculum emphasis in the context of their goals and aspirations. Any revisions?

▶

Reread your summary of the learners' "significant others." Consider your beliefs about learning and motivation in context. Any revisions?

▶

5. *The Cooperating Teacher.* Reread your analysis of the cooperating teacher's perspective. What are the points of conflict between your initial perspective and the cooperating teacher's perspective? Why do you think these differences exist? Years of experience? Age? Training? Background factors? Reconsider your own perspective again. Do you have any second thoughts about it?

▶

TRACING ORIGINS

We are obviously not born with perspectives on teaching. Where do they come from? By tracing our beliefs back to their origins, we are in a better position to examine their validity. The beliefs become less taken for granted as we identify their sources. We have discussed some of the sources for a perspective in Chapter 6. Reread your analyses of your experiences as a learner and as a teacher (Chapter 6).

To what extent have these past experiences affected your initial perspective? What other significant experiences have made an impact on your perspective? In what ways?

▶

Did your family's attitude toward teaching or toward education influence your perspective? What about the way you or your brothers and sisters were treated as children by your parents?

▶

What about your professional training? Have the values expressed by faculty members or by your fellow students influenced your perspective? In what ways?

▶

CONSIDERING CONSEQUENCES

The saying "actions speak louder than words" might well have been written to describe the effects of teaching. Any teacher's perspective, if implemented, has consequences for learners. Teachers act in certain ways based on their beliefs and on contextual constraints, and learners interpret the teacher's action in both intended and unintended ways. The unintended meanings learners derive from a teacher's actions are part of the school's "hidden curriculum."[3] For example, a female teacher in a working-class community school keeps a tight control over pupils' classroom behavior, requiring permission before any learner may speak and keeping all children in their seats except when she gives them bathroom passes. She presents the subject matter through a lecture-recitation method, emphasizing rote memorization of the facts as she or the textbook present them. The children are always kept busy in class, and their homework consists of worksheets with detailed instructions to follow. Promptness, neatness, effort, and compliance with instructions are highly emphasized. The teacher makes a point of publicly displaying the individual pupil's work that most successfully meets these criteria.

Another female teacher works in a school whose community is dominated by the research and development (R&D) division of a large electronics corporation. She allows a great deal of movement in her classroom: children speak to her and to their classmates without raising hands; different activities are located around the room with children moving from one to another at will; children leave the room to visit the bathroom or learning center without passes. Most of the children engage either in projects during class time with the teacher acting as a resource person, or in small discussion sessions with the teacher acting as a facilitator. Children actively question and criticize sources of information and learn to derive their own conclusions from the available evidence. Independent and logical thinking, problem-solving ability, and creativity seem to be what this teacher looks for in the children's work. Children are encouraged to work cooperatively on the projects they select together and the teacher tries to use inherent interest in projects as the primary motivation.

What might be the differences between the messages that pupils in these two different classrooms receive?

▶

Now apply a similar analysis to your own initial perspective. Try to identify the messages or meanings the learners are likely to take from your beliefs if and when you implement them.[4] Consider both intended and unintended meanings, both short- and long-term effects.

The following sets of questions illustrate this approach to the analysis of your initial perspective for possible consequences. They are only examples.

- **Diversity of Learners.** Would you treat different groups of learners differently? Would this differential treatment affect any groups' ability or desire to assume particular social roles in the future?
- **Learning.** Would your emphasis be on the kind of motivation that grades or personal recognition generate, or on the inherent interest learners derive from work they choose to do? What would be the

likelihood of the learners' motivation continuing beyond the school years and outside the school walls? How would the learners likely view the subject matter you teach?

- **Role of Teacher and Control.** What views on authority would the learners likely derive from your role as a teacher and the patterns of control you develop? Would they view authority as arbitrary or reasonable, based on power or on competence, absolute or negotiable?
- **School and Society.** From the example you set for the learners, would they be inclined to attempt to change the social order or try to adjust to it? Would they be inclined to participate actively in the political process or to allow others to do it for them? Would they be inclined to acquiesce to authority or to assess independently the validity of claims?
- **Knowledge.** Would the learners be inclined to view school subject matter as absolute or tentative, value-neutral or value-laden, useful for interpreting their own everyday experience or primarily for academic matters, comprehensible as an integrated whole or as a set of compartmentalized subjects or topics within subjects?

Although questions such as these are difficult for you to answer before having had a great deal of teaching experience, jot down any answers you can give to any of these questions.
▶

Reread your responses in this section. Do they cause you to reconsider any aspects of your perspective? Write down any reservations you now have about your perspective.
▶

GOALS

Chapter 2 discussed the goals or priorities that you set for yourself as a *student* teacher. This section will help you use your thinking about your perspective to develop the goals or priorities that you, as a student *teacher,* set for your learners. These latter goals will serve as a guide to your teaching.

Are Goals Necessary?

Education is a purposeful activity. If it has no direction, it is unlikely to be successful. Without direction it is even difficult to decide what should count as success.

The same can be said of teaching. One of the major differences between teaching and other interpersonal interactions, such as baby-sitting, is that teaching has direction. If someone is unable or unwilling to guide an ineraction toward some growth or learning, then it is not proper to call that interaction "teaching." Field experiences can be found in many sites: schools, 4-H, Boy Scouts, Girl Scouts, nursing homes, prison, Big Brother/ Big Sister programs, and many more. Whether they count as "teaching" field experiences depends on the appropriateness of someone giving direction or guidance to the interpersonal interaction. In schools everybody expects the teacher to take responsibility for the learning of the students. In other settings also people may expect or want some degree of "teaching." On the other hand, the situation may call only for a person to be someone's friend or to keep someone company.

To force "teaching" on someone who does not want it in a situation that does not call for it or to avoid the teacher's role when the situation requires it are both common faults of students beginning their initial field experiences. Students do not always give the appropriate amount of direction to the interactions they have with their clients or pupils.

What Are Some Tentative Goals?

Your initial perspective has already touched on many issues related to goals. By formulating your initial statement of perspective you were, in part, setting goals for your teaching.

Each dimension—that is, each of the six basic issues—is related to goals of teaching. Each issue raises questions about goals which your perspective might have addressed. By revisiting your perspective you might gain another basis for revising or expanding your goals.

Control. Who really sets the goals, and who do you think should: the administration, textbook publishers, the state, the cooperating teacher or you? How sensitive should you be to learner interests?
▶

Diversity. Should you apply the same goals to all the learners regardless of their backgrounds or abilities?
▶

Teacher's Role. Is it important for the learners to develop certain attitudes or feelings toward you as the teacher, such as trust, respect, or honesty?
▶

Learning. Is it important for you to develop a sense of group identity? Should cooperative, competitive, or individualist attitudes be developed? Should you try to develop an interest in the subject matter, and how important is this interest? Should you try to develop a sense of the whole, or should the emphasis be on a set of building blocks of knowledge skills?
▶

Knowledge. What is more important to learn, process-type knowledge, such as inquiry, problem solving, and creativity, or content-type knowledge, such as facts, concepts, and principles? Should you help learners to construct their own interpretation of the content or to learn the "accepted" view? Do you want learners to view knowledge as certain or as tentative?
▶

School and Society. Are you trying to help the learners adjust to or integrate into the current social order, or to provide them "with the knowledge, attitudes, or skills to deal critically and creatively with that reality in order to improve it"?[5]
▶

If you have not done so up to this point, state your goals for the field experience. What do you want to accomplish? In what ways do you intend the field experience to benefit the learner(s)?

Reviewing Goals

You might want to review your goals. For example, you could do the following exercises:

1. Determine if they are realistic. Can you implement them in this school with this cooperating teacher?
▶

2. Sort them out into short- and long-term goals. For each long-term goal, you could make sure you also have something immediate at which to aim. For each short-term goal, decide if it is an end in

itself or a means to an end. If the latter case applies, what is the more ultimate end? Was this end included as one of your goals?

▶

3. For each goal try to identify one or two sample indicators (i.e., things to look for that indicate the goal is achieved).

▶

4. Next to each goal write 1, 2, or 3 to indicate the priority you assign to it. Let 1 signify that the goal is essential and that you would consider your teaching a failure if it were not largely achieved. Let 2 signify that the goal is very important but that you still would consider your teaching worthwhile for the pupils, even if you achieve only partial success toward this goal. Let 3 signify that the goal would be nice to achieve but is far from essential. Your success as a teacher does not depend on your success with this goal. Now you might want to write down your 1-rated goals here. These will receive the highest priority in your field experience.

▶

Having considered your goals in terms of feasibility, long- and short-term implications, indicators of achievement, and priorities, you might find it necessary to make revisions. If so, do it here.

▶

The goals you have set are only tentative. As you proceed in your field experience, you will undoubtedly have to make midcourse corrections. Goals that initially seem to be straightforward and clearly important may need to be modified or replaced. For example, a learner's math problem may turn out to be a motivational problem, and the teacher would have to adjust goals accordingly.

Not only should goals be modified when necessary, they should also be suspended at times. You should expect to encounter situations in which your goals have to be put aside while you deal with other more pressing problems or capitalize on opportune moments. For example, a teacher may want to postpone teaching how to analyze a poem, if the learners just experienced a violent situation in the school, watched a controversial television program, or are excited about an upcoming election.

Goals can guide teaching without placing a stranglehold on it. The key is flexibility in their selection and use.

NOTES

1. George Kelly, *The Psychology of Personal Constructs,* Vol. 2 (New York: W. W. Norton, 1955), p. 560.
2. This inventory was adapted from an instrument developed by Zeichner and Tabachnick at the University of Wisconsin–Madison.
3. Philip Jackson, *Life in Classrooms* (New York: Holt, Rinehart and Winston, 1968).
4. Carl Grant and Kenneth Zeichner, "On Becoming a Reflective Teacher," in *Preparing for Reflective Teaching,* ed. Carl A. Grant (Boston: Allyn and Bacon, 1984), p. 15.
5. Ibid.

PART 4
Planning to Teach

CHAPTER 9

Why Should Anyone Learn Your Subject Matter?

The question in this chapter's title may seem impertinent. It certainly did to me when on my first day of teaching a student asked, "Why should anyone learn this stuff?" Since I had no answer, I told the student to be quiet; he was, and the questioned remained unanswered. However, as the days wore on, the question nagged at me. It was, after all, a good question, no matter what the student's motive was for asking it. We should know why we are taking people's time and consuming the community's resources for teaching language arts, social studies, math, science, physical education, vocational education, foreign languages, computer science, home economics, industrial arts, and all the other subjects. At the very least, we ought to know why anyone should learn the particular subject matter we teach.

IMPORTANCE OF YOUR SUBJECT MATTER

EXERCISE 9.1 Most and Least Important Courses Taken

Think back over your schooling career. Try to identify the five courses or subjects you studied that in retrospect seem most important. Do the same for those you consider least important. *Webster's New World Dictionary* defines *important* as "meaning a great deal; having much significance, consequence or value." The less important, the more trivial, time-wasting, and fruitless.

FORM 9.1 MOST AND LEAST IMPORTANT COURSES

Most Important	Least Important
1.	
2.	
3.	
4.	
5.	

When I try this exercise with large heterogeneous classes of undergraduates, I receive two lists that are almost identical. That is, every subject that someone considers most important someone else considers least important. My conclusion is that no subject will get universal support. A lot depends on the particular learner.

For each course you listed, examine your reasons for putting it in the column you did.

What criteria for selecting subject matter do your choices imply? Consider the following possibilities.[1]

1. *Context.* Are your choices based on their contribution to further learning (formal or nonformal), to your vocation, or personal–social living? That is, are your choices based on *what* they are useful for?
2. *Further learning.* For those choices related to further learning, are any important because they provide "basic tools" for further learning, or because they offer fundamental ideas (i.e., key concepts or broadly applicable explanations)?
3. *Vocation.* For those choices related to your vocation (or avocation), are any important because they contributed to selection, performance, or upgrading of your vocation/avocation?
4. *Personal–social living.* Are any of your choices based on their contribution to the society or community as a whole while others are based on their contribution to you as an individual? That is, are your choices based on *who* (i.e., society or individual) is supposed to benefit from them?
5. *Use situations.* Are any of your choices based on the frequency or diversity of situations in which you put them to use or how crucial (though possibly rare or unique) the situation is when they are put to use? That is, are your choices based on their *situational usefulness?*
6. *Timing.* Are any of your choices important or unimportant because they are useful at the present time, in the foreseeable future, or in the remote future? That is, are your choices based on *when* they are useful?

7. *Use mode.* Do your choices reflect an emphasis on using knowledge to solve the types of problems and perform the kinds of skills similar to those taught (e.g., vocational training, reading), to provide ideas that enable you to interpret the social and natural world in which you live (e.g., physics), or to provide imagery and other associations that enrich experience (e.g., poetry)?

If these questions help you uncover some of the implicit reasons you value certain subject matter over others, try jotting down these insights here.
▶

Many of these assumptions about education might underlie your justification for teaching your own subject matter. However, personal history plays a role also.

EXERCISE 9.2   The Road to My Subject Matter

Think back over your life, both in and out of school. Jot down significant events (e.g., a trip to Europe) or people (e.g., a brother-in-law who is a scientist) that have influenced the value you place on your subject matter.

FORM 9.2 KEY EVENTS AND PEOPLE

Events	People

Together, your general perspective on education and your personal history have contributed greatly to your decision to teach your subject matter. What is even more important is that these two factors have influenced your justification for someone else's learning it. If this justification affected only your answer to learners' questions about the value of your subject matter, it would be important to consider very seriously. Not to be able to answer such questions is not only embarrassing but also irresponsible.

However, your justification is important for another reason. How you justify your subject matter suggests what approach you will use and what emphasis you will give. Consider the case of science teaching. Here are six reasons for teaching science.[2] For each justification I mention the particular emphasis one would expect to find and an example of that emphasis on science curriculum development.

1. **Everyday Coping**

   Justification: Science is useful for coping with our problems.

   Emphasis: Students must learn how to apply scientific principles to our technological and natural environment.

   Example: Courses that examine the scientific basis for technological advances (e.g., the physics of the internal combustion engine), or aim at using science to develop solutions to social problems (e.g., environmental studies).

2. **Structure of Science**

   Justification: Science is an intellectually exciting form of inquiry in which students will engage.

   Emphasis: Students must actively engage in real scientific inquiry themselves during which they examine the interplay between theory and evidence, the adequacy of particular models used to explain physical phenomena, and the tentativeness of scientific knowledge.

   Example: Many curricula developed during the 1960s, such as PSSC physics, BSCS biology, CHEM Study chemistry, and Man: A Course of Study in social studies.

3. **Scientific Skill Development**

   Justification: Science education develops basic skills such as measuring, observing, hypothesizing, categorizing, and controlling variables.

   Emphasis: Science is viewed as a set of skills to be learned rather than as knowledge to be acquired, i.e., process- rather than product-oriented.

   Example: Science—A Process Approach (i.e., AAAS elementary science).

4. **Correct Explanations**

   Justification: The purpose of science education is the transmission of our cultural heritage.

Emphasis: Clear explanations by teachers and acceptance of ideas by students.

Example: Many science courses based on listening to lectures and/or reading textbooks.

5. **Solid Foundations**

   Justification: Science education at a particular level prepares students for the next level.

   Emphasis: Mastery of content.

   Example: Most introductory courses that serve as prerequisites to more advanced courses.

6. **Self as Explainer**

   Justification: Science is a cultural institution, through which humans express their need to explain and demonstrate their capability for rational inquiry.

   Emphasis: Science education, according to this view, examines the growth and change in scientific ideas as a function of human purposes and historical settings.

   Example: Harvard Project Physics.

It should be clear that none of these approaches is correct and none is incorrect. Each might be "right" in a particular situation, that is, with particular learners, in a particular context, and with a particular teacher.

Your own justification and emphasis need not and probably will not rely on any one "pure" type. Most of us are eclectics, particularly once we realize the complexities of real classrooms in real schools.

EXERCISE 9.3   Justifying Your Own Subject Matter

Try to generate a set of possible answers to the question:

Why study your subject matter at all?

See if you can come up with five to ten possible answers. Do not worry if your answers overlap slightly.

►

Now for each justification describe one or more emphases that derive from it.

►

Finally, write a statement describing the justification and emphases which you believe underlies your teaching (i.e., your approach to your subject matter) in your specific field experience.

▶

ANALYSIS OF JUSTIFICATION AND EMPHASIS

Any approach to subject matter represents a resolution (however tentative) to a set of dilemmas or issues any teacher faces. We discussed six of these issues earlier at great length (see particularly Chapter 7). Here we shall return to a subset of the six basic issues in order to analyze your approach and thereby to consider your perspective on teaching from another angle. After reviewing Chapter 7, particularly the sections on learning and motivation, school and society, knowledge, and diversity of learners, try to analyze your approach according to the following questions:

1. *Learning and Motivation*
   Does your approach imply any theory of learning and motivation? If so, does it imply a behavioristic or a cognitive theory? For example, does it emphasize learning to perform a set of observable behaviors based on a system of rewards and incentives (as in the Scientific-Skill-Development approach) or learning a coherent framework of scientific conceptions by a process similar to that in which scientists engage (as in the Structure-of-Science approach)?

▶

2. *School and Society*
   What relationship between school knowledge and the society outside of school does your approach imply? For example, does it imply a role in which the school maintains the status quo by transmitting the cultural heritage and helping students to adjust to the current state of affairs (as in the Correct-Explanations approach), or do they imply a role in which the school helps society become aware of and solve social and technological problems (as in the Everyday-Coping approach)?

▶

3. *Knowledge*
   What assumptions about knowledge does your approach imply? For example, does it imply that knowledge is something constructed

by people in social settings (as in the Self-as-Explainer approach) or that knowledge is certain and students must only acquire it (as in the Correct-Explanations and Solid-Foundations approaches)?

▶

4. *Diversity of Learners*
Would your approach depend on the type of learners whom you might teach? For example, might you treat learners of "lower ability" differently (i.e., based on different assumptions about learning and motivation, knowledge, and relation of school knowledge to societal roles) than learners of "higher ability"?

▶

Does your analysis of your justification and emphasis (i.e., your approach) suggest any additions to or revisions of either your initial perspective or goals (see Chapter 8)? If so, note these changes here.

NOTES

1. Adapted from M. Johnson, *Intentionality in Education* (Albany, N.Y.: Center for Curriculum Research and Services, 1977), pp. 134–135.
2. Adapted from Douglas Roberts, "Developing the Concept of 'Curriculum Emphasis' in Science Education," *Science Education* 60(2), 1982.

CHAPTER 10

What and How Do You Plan to Teach?

At various times during your teacher education program you will have opportunities to teach lessons all on your own. These opportunities, whether they occur in one-to-one tutoring or one-to-large group teaching situations, will allow you to find out how it feels to be responsible for someone else's learning. Observing classes and assisting teachers are valuable field experiences, but being the one that sets the pace, the one to whom learners look for direction and clarification, and the one who bears the responsibility for the success or failure of the lesson adds another dimension in your gradual transition from student to teacher. This chapter is intended to help you prepare for these experiences. This preparation increases the chances that both you and the learners will derive maximum benefit from the experience.

The key to the preparation of a lesson is careful planning. You may have studied lesson planning previously, perhaps in a "methods" course. The purpose of this chapter is not so much to teach you how to plan lessons as it is to help you reflect on your plans. The more experienced you become, the more this reflection will become automatic. As a teacher in training, you will benefit from deliberate and explicit reflection on your lesson plans.

Although lesson plans are recommended by most educators, they disagree regarding what elements lesson plans should include. Let us examine the range of planning elements recommended by educators.

DIRECTION

Most educators claim that lesson planning must be given a general sense of direction. Direction includes the tasks learners are supposed to confront and how the learners are expected to change as a consequence.

Activities

The heart of any lesson is the set of activities that you arrange for the learners. In fact, much of classroom teaching can be considered the management of activities.

I have found it useful to think about any learning activity as a task in which teachers expect learners to engage.[1] Tasks include (but are not limited to) the following:

1. Solving math problems
2. Taking lecture notes
3. Observing properties of an object
4. Writing essays
5. Predicting physical changes
6. Performing musical compositions
7. Looking up information in reference books
8. Debating social issues
9. Playing roles
10. Reading stories
11. Following directions
12. Reviewing facts previously learned

One important common feature of all these tasks is that they are all things in which the *learners,* rather than the teachers, are expected to engage. That is, these are the tasks that we want learners to accomplish. As teachers, we select or design a task on the basis of its potential for resulting in significant learning and its appropriateness for our learners.

Although describing activities in terms of learner tasks is generally useful, you may find that this approach does not work well for certain types of lessons. If your lesson is highly teacher-dominated (e.g., lecture or demonstration) and you expect the learners primarily to listen to what you say or watch what you do, then you will likely want your activity described in terms of teacher tasks rather than learner tasks.

Objectives

For a task to be educational, it must lead to learning. Therefore, an important criterion in selecting or designing tasks is their potential for resulting in significant learning. There are certainly other relevant criteria for tasks, such as the extent to which they provide challenge, enjoyment, and a cooperative atmosphere. However important these criteria may be, the primary basis for a task's educative value is the residue of learning that remains after learners engage in it.

Much has already been written about objectives in education (probably too much!). Some people advocate expressing objectives in terms of observable behaviors learners are expected to exhibit after instruction.[2] Others disagree, preferring a more permissive vocabulary which includes internal changes in students. These people suggest we use verbs like "know" and "understand" in our objectives as well as flowcharts and networks of concepts as expressions of learning objectives.[3] I will leave the matter of form for objectives to the person in charge of your field experience.

At a minimum you should consider two sorts of objectives: capabilities and ideas. The former describes what learners should be able to do after the lesson that they could not do before it. The latter captures the main concepts, facts, or generalizations which learners should memorize, become more familiar with, or understand as a consequence of the lesson. You may also want to consider attitudes, although changing deeply held attitudes is typically not feasible in a single lesson.

Most people assume that objectives are the logical place to begin when planning a lesson. As they say, you must know where you are going before you can decide how to get there, or you must know what you are trying to produce before you can decide how to produce it. Travel and factory metaphors are very persuasive but, of course, they are only metaphors. Education is neither a trip nor an assembly line. Often we can decide what the likely educational benefit of a lesson will be only after planning some of its details. It is less important *when* objectives are considered than *that* objectives are considered. Therefore, my point here is that you give serious consideration to the skills, knowledge, and attitudes you expect students to learn, rather than when or how you do it.

One piece of advice about objectives—try to limit your lesson to one or, at most, two important objectives. There can be many possible benefits of a lesson, but just as in successful public speaking, we can rarely make more than one or two major points at one time. Learners have limited abilities to remember, understand, and acquire competence in any subject matter. People who try to accomplish too much risk not accomplishing anything.

Entry Characteristics

> If I had to reduce all of educational psychology to just one principle I would say this: The most important single factor influencing learning is what the learner already knows. Ascertain this and teach him accordingly.[4]

Whether cognitive psychologists like David Ausubel, talking about "prior knowledge," or behavioral psychologists talking about "entry behaviors,'' educational psychologists insist that lessons take into account the skills and understandings that learners bring to any educational activity. However, finding out the levels that learners are at and then not leaving them there is easier said than done. Methods for determining what learners know, believe, and can do include observations, interviews, analysis of test performance, and products of the learners' work.

Observations provide the opportunity to gain information about learners as they interact with their physical and social environment. How they manipulate objects and what they say to their peers are of particular interest.

Interviews enable us to probe the learners' thoughts about content. By beginning interviews with a stimulus like a picture, a memorable quotation, or a physical phenomenon, and then asking the learner to react to the stimulus by providing an explanation, prediction, or evaluation, we increase our understanding of the learner's ideas and, particularly, misconceptions.

Careful analysis of test results tells us not only how competent the learners are but also what problems exist. The key to diagnosis is a detailed study of learners' mistakes. All too often we treat mistakes or tests as things to mark wrong rather than as sources of insight into the learner's thought processes.

Lab reports, essays, problem sets, and other completed assignments are clues to the way learners have interpreted tasks teachers have given to them. It is not unusual for teachers to present tasks to learners on the assumption that they have the requisite skills and understanding. When learners do not write the kinds of lab reports or essays or solve problem sets as expected, the reason may be that they have taken a task that they cannot handle and have reinterpreted it into one they can manage. In such a case, analysis of an inadequately accomplished task may provide a window into the learner's internal resources.

SPECIFICS

The next three elements provide the details of the lesson plan. Here the plan specifies what the teacher and the learners will do, say, cover and produce. Although any lesson plan might include a content outline, a set of procedures, and the expected results, different sorts of lessons will focus on different elements. For example, a plan for a lecture might highlight the content outline, a plan for a role play might stress procedures, and a plan for laboratory work might emphasize the expected experimental results. On the other hand, a discussion might include elaborate plans for all three elements.

Content Outline

Whenever teachers prepare lectures or other activities intended to cover a body of content, they usually find it helpful to plan major topics and subtopics. Decisions include how much and what content to cover, what examples, anecdotes, and applications to include, and how to organize and sequence the content.

One of the most common mistakes of beginning teachers is to attempt to cover too much content at one time. Sticking to an overambitious content outline can result in rushing through the lesson, squelching learners' questions, and treating topics superficially. It is one thing to plan more than one really needs, just to be safe, and another to put students under excessive content coverage pressure in order to stick to the plan.

Experienced teachers have a wealth of anecdotes and examples in their repertoire which they can use to illustrate their points. Beginning teachers (and even many experienced teachers) need to plan these illustrations ahead of time. Good examples are among the most valuable teaching tools for helping learners understand and remember content. Therefore, it is worth the time to think examples through ahead of time.

Presentations in which one idea builds on another and in which topics exhibit a sensible progression are most likely to hold learner interest and give a coherent view of the subject matter. In outlining the content, consider whether to sequence content from most to least familiar, from general to specific (or vice versa), from simple to complex, in chronological order, according to steps of procedure, from least to most difficult, from closest to farthest, from smallest to largest, according to prerequisite order, according to the method of inquiry, or some other reasonable sequence. It is important to choose a sequence that will keep students interested, represent the subject matter in a sensible manner, and help learners understand specific content as part of a larger whole.

Procedures

Lesson planning requires more than simply providing a curriculum framework. It also entails putting instructional flesh on the curriculum bones.[5]

In Chapter 5 you read about (and perhaps developed) a lesson profile. Those ideas are as relevant to lesson planning as they were to classroom observation. To reiterate, any planned activity has a well-defined beginning, a middle, and an ending. The beginning might include settling down, distributing papers or other materials, introducing the activity, giving instructions before work begins, or relating the new lesson to the previous lesson. The middle might include any of the tasks listed earlier in the "Activities" section. The ending might include review, conclusions, cleaning up the room, writing up or sharing results, and debriefing learners (e.g., what does each learner think he or she learned?).

In planning the details of the lesson, consider the inclusion of each of the following:

Questions. Discussions are typically most effective when they are guided by a set of prepared questions. This is obvious to anyone who has watched a moderator guide a television panel discussion. Questions are equally effective in getting learners to think about statements made in a lecture, results obtained in a demonstration or laboratory experiment, phenomena observed on a field trip, or experiences obtained outside of class. Planning in advance provides an opportunity to think through the kinds of response learners might generate, giving the teacher some basis for revision. For example, "why" and "what if" questions may be more likely to generate thought than "what" and "who" questions.

Transitions. When there is more than one activity for a lesson, the transition between activities requires planning. The logistics may be complex and time-consuming. Regaining the learners' attention and getting the learners to cognitively shift gears is difficult at any grade level.

Pitfalls. Being forewarned is being forearmed. Giving some thought to what can go wrong in the lesson may prevent a disaster. Any lesson can have undesirable side effects;[6] by anticipating possible false conclusions or negative attitudes, the teacher can often prevent them. Procedures that may be unsafe, wasteful, or counterproductive can sometimes be identified ahead of time and the learners warned about them. Obviously, knowledge of pitfalls increases with experience, but even the beginning teacher can try to anticipate problems.

Results

Whenever a lesson consists of an activity that leads to answers, products, or experimental results, the teacher can try to anticipate these outcomes. One way to do this is to try the activity alone in advance. Doing the laboratory experiment or demonstration and observing the results, writing the composition from the instructions, solving the problems while thinking aloud, allows the teacher to troubleshoot the procedure (see "Pitfalls") and to be able to plan questions and comments which help learners get the point.

Although content, procedures, and results are presented as separate elements, in lesson planning these three elements can be planned in one integrated section. For example, in a demonstration-lecture the teacher might demonstrate key points of the lecture with an experiment and follow each experimental result obtained with a question presented to the learners. In such a case the teacher might want to coordinate content, procedures, and results.

PROVISIONS

The teacher has to provide many things for the learners in order to make certain that the lesson is successful. These provisions include resources, opportunities for feedback, sufficient time, and follow-up activities.

Resources

Much of the actual lesson planning time is taken by preparing and providing resources for the activities. Resources may include written material, audiovisuals, and manipulatives. Resources may be handed out to individuals or to groups, placed in a central location (e.g., a learning center or bulletin board), or kept by the teacher.

Written material includes books, worksheets, bibliographies, outlines, assignment sheets, data record sheets, paragraphs or poems, or notes. To prepare them, the teacher may actually have to write them, make dittos from a teacher's guide, or simply assemble them.

Audiovisuals (AVs) include films, slide sets, filmstrips, videotapes or discs, audio tapes, records, overhead projections, charts, maps, and posters. For most AVs the teacher may not only have to obtain the material (by ordering or reserving it in advance), but may also have to provide the necessary equipment, and set it up in advance.

Manipulatives include laboratory equipment, props, paper, pencils, crayons, paints, scissors, string, and paste or glue. If learners are supposed to supply any of the manipulatives, someone will have to remind them to bring them in, and provide those items individuals forget.

In addition to preparing these resources, planning may include deciding how to distribute them. Much time can be lost during handouts if routines for distributing materials have not been established.

One further resource to consider is space. How to arrange chairs, tables, and desks can affect greatly both the effectiveness of the activity and the type of classroom climate. In a sense, the teacher's planning sets the stage for a lesson.

Opportunities for Feedback

The saying "practice makes perfect" is only half true. Practice is crucial for developing competence, but practice without feedback tends to reinforce mistakes and inefficient procedures. Feedback regarding performance allows people to make adjustments which, over time, lead to improvement, if not perfection. At least two types of feedback are necessary: feedback to the teacher and feedback to the learners.

The teacher can profit from feedback about how comprehensible the material was, how smoothly the lesson went, what the learners gained from the lesson, or any number of things. Debriefing sessions at the conclusion of the lesson (e.g., asking the class "What do you think you learned from this lesson?") are one means for gaining feedback. Other methods include brief questionnaires, random exit interviews, quizzes, and analyses of student products (see "Entry Characteristics").

The learners also need feedback. Some tasks have feedback built in (e.g., it is obvious to the learner when he or she successfully rides a bike). Programmed instruction and many computer-assisted programs build feedback into the activity. In other cases, short quizzes corrected in class, examplars of products (e.g., a model A+ essay), teacher demonstrations, and presentations of typical errors all provide feedback when it cannot be built in. In most cases feedback should be accompanied by a rationale, in order to increase the likelihood that the learners will accept the feedback.

Timing

Although time is actually a resource (and the most precious one at that!), we treat it separately here because of its importance. As was mentioned earlier, most beginning teachers are overambitious in the amount they plan for their lessons. That is, they underestimate the time required to complete an activity.

One way to minimize this risk is for the teacher to go through the procedure in advance (see "Pitfalls" in the "Procedures" section). An additional way is to make time allotments for each step of the procedure, estimating both maximum and minimum completion times. Still another way is to build in extra time with optional activities to provide for stragglers, mistakes, and miscalculations. Finally, the teacher can prioritize certain topics or procedures in order to have some basis for paring down the lesson once it is in progress. By considering priorities in advance, the teacher can avoid having to leave a lesson unfinished, particularly when the whole lesson culminates in the final topic or step.

Follow-up

Lessons that continue beyond a single school day and beyond a single classroom's walls are most likely to have a lasting impact on learners. The teacher can provide for follow-up by relating the day's lesson to a future one, to one in another class, to current events, or to an upcoming television show or movie. The teacher can also provide for follow-up by giving a homework assignment which gives additional practice (with feedback) of a learned skill, or helps the learner transfer the learning to other situations.

Whatever follow-up the teacher plans, allowing sufficient time for explaining it, providing written records to remind learners of it, and communicating to learners that it is important (e.g., that it "counts") all contribute to the long-term impact of the lesson.

EXERCISE 10.1 A Preliminary Plan

Using as many of the preceding ten planning elements as you can, jot down some initial ideas for a lesson. In generating ideas, consider the following factors:

The teacher: If you are assisting a teacher (i.e., as a student teacher or as an assistant teacher), what is the teacher working on with the learners? That is, what is the teacher trying to accomplish, and how can your lesson contribute to this cooperative effort?

▶

The subject matter: What are some crucial ideas or skills in the subject matter you teach? Can you think of some effective way of teaching any of these important things?

▶

The learners. Are the learners currently interested in something that you can specially incorporate into a lesson? Are they deficient in some skill or in their understanding of some idea?

▶

Context: What is going on in the world, nation, state, community, or school that might be incorporated into the lesson or that has implications for your objectives?

▶

With these initial ideas in mind, you can do some preliminary planning of a lesson. At this point all that is necessary is a set of preliminary answers to the ten questions listed earlier. The preliminary planning sheet is given below as a guide to this process.

FORM 10.1 PRELIMINARY PLANNING SHEET

Planning element	Planning question	Preliminary answers (plans)
I. Direction		
1. Activity	What activity do you plan to initiate or lead?	
2. Objectives	What are the students supposed to learn from the activity?	
3. Entry characteristics	What prior skills and understandings do you expect the learners to bring to the lesson?	
II. Specifics (use separate sheet for specifics as necessary)		
4. Content	What specific contents will you cover?	
5. Procedures	What specifically will you and the learners do during the activity?	
6. Results	What results do you expect?	
III. Provisions		
7. Resources	What facilities and materials will you and the learners need in order to carry out the activity?	
8. Feedback	How will you and the learners be provided with feedback regarding their progress?	
9. Time	How long will the activity take?	
10. Follow-up	What activities will you assign as a means of extending or reinforcing the lesson?	

REFINING PRELIMINARY PLANS

Planning a lesson entails tentatively resolving a set of planning dilemmas. That is, as you refine your preliminary plans, you will confront many issues, some of which we discussed in the context of your perspective on teaching. Just as Chapter 9 focused on a subset of the six basic issues, so too does this chapter. Here we shall consider issues concerning control, learning, teacher role, and diversity as they relate to lesson planning.

Control

Who should decide what, what should be the bases for decisions, and how stringently should decisions be enforced are the sorts of planning dilemmas teachers face regarding control. Activities, content, resources, time, procedures, feedback, and objectives must be selected, developed, or allocated by someone or some group (e.g., the teacher, the textbook publisher, the state or school district, or the students themselves). This planning must be based on learner, teacher, or community interest, on teacher background or competence, on resource availability, on the structure of the subject matter, on the school's goals, or on tradition. For example, the pacing decision of when to move on to the next topic or activity may be based on a predetermined schedule (decided by the teacher in advance), on the teacher's perception of when a particular learner or group of learners is reading (the "steering group"[7]), or on the initiative of individual learners. Therefore, while refining your preliminary plans you might consider who will control the direction and flow of your lesson and how the lesson, in turn, will control the behavior of the learners.

Teacher Role

As you plan the activities, procedures, objectives, feedback, and follow-up, you are adopting (perhaps unconsciously) a particular role for yourself as the teacher. In particular, your plans set the stage for you to act as a transmitter of information, facilitator of group dynamics, an adversary, an expert in an apprenticeship situation, a student, a scientist, an advocate, a manager, or any number of other roles. Therefore, before finalizing your lesson plan you might want to consider the role you would feel most comfortable in, the role that would be most effective, and the role that would be most appropriate for the particular school, classroom, cooperating teacher, and students.

Learning and Motivation

You can think of your lesson plan as an expression of your views on learning and motivation. That is, planning a lesson entails a tentative resolution of dilemmas related to how people learn and what motivates them to learn. For example, you could consider whether the lesson plan suggests a learning process that is active or passive, rote or meaningful, internal or external, intrinsically or extrinsically motivated, individually or group-based, cooperative or competitive, and primarily cognitive or affective. By referring to these dichotomies as planning dilemmas, I want to underscore the idea that there is no right or wrong and that these dichotomies are not mutually exclusive. The situation (i.e., the particular subject matter, teacher, learners, and context) defines planning options.

Diversity of Learners

Until now the discussion of lesson plans has implied one plan for the whole class. Since most classes are composed of a diversity of learners, however, lesson plans may have to be adjusted to individual differences. The plans you have prepared thus far reflect the extent and type of adjustments you want to make. Lesson plans may not only provide opportunities to discover how diverse the class is and to group learners on the basis of this information, but also be a guide for the preparation of activities, procedures, objectives, and resources appropriate for different learners or groups of learners. In a sense, a lesson plan expresses the teacher's views about the individualization of instruction.

With your preliminary lesson plan in front of you and with these general comments about control, teacher role, learning, and diversity in mind, you can review your plan and make any revisions that seem important to you as you reconsider it.

REFLECTIONS ON PLANNING

Has your lesson planning caused you to reconsider either your initial perspective or goals (refer to Chapter 8)? Use this opportunity to jot down your thoughts here.
▶

EXERCISE 10.2   A Postmortem

Events rarely proceed as planned. After you have taught your lesson, reconsider your plans. In doing so, you may find the following questions useful:

1. Did the *activity* you planned actually occur? If not, why not?
2. Were your *objectives* realistic? Did other ones emerge during the lesson?
3. Did the *learners' actual knowledge and skills* correspond to your expectations? Did any discrepancies cause you to modify the lesson?

4. Did you cover what you planned? Did you plan too much or too little *content* to cover?
5. Did the *procedures* work? If not, what went wrong?
6. Did the *results* you anticipated occur? If not, what went wrong?
7. Did you provide sufficient *resources?* What else was needed?
8. Did you get adequate *feedback* on the lesson? What did you learn from the feedback? Did the learners get sufficient feedback?
9. Was the *time* adequate? Was the time used efficiently?
10. Were the *follow-up* activities done? Were they effective?

By answering these questions, you are conducting a "postmortem" of your lesson. After reflecting on each planning element, you might think of ways to improve the lesson.

CONCLUSIONS

Planning never really ends. Plans are modified during the lesson. After the lesson is taught, plans are made for the next lesson. Lesson planning is never completed. One can never fully anticipate what will actually occur during a lesson. Therefore, people typically find it necessary to modify plans while teaching, and to rethink plans after teaching.

> You are not necessarily a better teacher simply for being able to predict your actions. The difficulty is in responding with some sensitivity to the situations you have engineered, because it is too easy, having *established* the situations, to feel responsible and protective towards them.[8] (Italics in original)

NOTES

1. See George Posner, "A Cognitive Science Conception of Curriculum and Instruction," *Journal of Curriculum Studies* 14(4) (1982), pp. 343–351; Walter Doyle, "Academic Work," *Review of Education Research* 53 (2), 1983.
2. See, for example, Robert Mager, *Preparing Instructional Objectives* (Palo Alto, Calif.: Fearon, 1962).
3. See, for example, George Posner and Alan Rudnitsky, *Course Design: A Guide to Curriculum Development for Teachers,* 2nd ed. (New York: Longman, 1981), Chapters 2 and 4.
4. David Ausubel, *Educational Psychology: A Cognitive View* (New York: Holt, Rinehart and Winston, 1968).

5. John Goodlad, *Planning and Organization for Teaching* (Washington, D.C.: National Education Association, 1965), p. 94.
6. Posner and Rudnitsky, op. cit., Chapter 8.
7. See Ulf Lundgren, "Frame Factors in Teaching," in *Curriculum and Instruction,* ed. Henry Giroux, Anthony Penna, and William Pinar (Berkeley, Calif.: McCutchan, 1981); Urban Dahllof, "Trends in Process-Related Research on Curriculum and Teaching at Different Problem Levels in Educational Sciences," in *Curriculum and Evaluation,* ed. Arno Bellack and Herbert Kliebard (Berkeley, Calif.: McCutchan, 1977).
8. Walker and Adelman, *A Guide to Classroom Observation* (see Chap. 3, n. 20).

PART 5
Revising Ideas

CHAPTER 11

What Have You Learned from Your Field Experience?

An experience is educational, if we learn something from it. If your field experience is to be educational, then it will have to help you learn something about teaching, about yourself, about learners, about your subject matter, or about the social milieu in which teaching occurs. This chapter is intended to help you crystallize some of the things you learned from your field experience thus far.

Your field experience has likely reinforced certain prior beliefs and challenged others, introduced you to new ways of thinking about some familiar things, and helped you find out more about teaching and your future in it. Now might be a good time to try to make that learning explicit.

Taking stock of learning (or anything else) is best done on paper. A progress report, whether written in the middle or at the end of a field experience, is one useful device for this purpose. Here you will find one approach to progress reports focusing on what you learned about teaching and, more specifically, on your perspective on teaching. Although I will suggest a particular format for this report, you or your college supervisor may prefer a different format. Obviously, you should follow whatever format is most appropriate to your own situation.

If you look for models to follow when writing your report, you will probably be surprised. Few books exist that provide a bridge between theory and practice. There are many books that present abstract ideas about what or how to teach and characteristics of a "good" teacher, drawing upon educational psychology, sociology, and philosophy as well as teaching experience. Also there are many books that offer purely anecdotal information about teaching.[1] However, few books exist that present principles, ideals, or issues about teaching, together with anecdotes for illustrative purposes.[2] Even fewer are written by teachers and present integrated perspectives on teaching together with anecdotal information.[3] Some of this sort do exist in fields other than teaching, such as in psychotherapy.[4]

In order to give you a clear idea of what a progress report might look like and how it serves as a bridge between theory and practice, I will suggest one possible format for a progress report and present in the Appendix some students' actual progress reports.

THE ANATOMY OF A PROGRESS REPORT

One format for progress reports that has proven useful contains the following questions:

1. What was (or is) the context of your field experience?
2. What were your goals for the field experience?
3. What did you learn about teaching in that situation (in terms of principles, ideals, or issues)?
4. What happened (in terms of episodes) during your field experience to cause you to learn those things?
5. How generalizable to other teaching situations are the things you learned?
6. How successful were you in achieving your goals?

Context

Introduce your progress report with two or three paragraphs about the situation in which your field experience is taking place. To do this, refer back to the situation analysis you wrote earlier (Chapters 4 and 5). As you did then, describe the school and community, then the cooperating teacher and the classroom. Try to write this section as background material for the reader. That is, set the stage for the drama that you will unfold.

Goals

Given this situation, what were your goals? Describe briefly the goals you set for yourself (refer to Chapter 2) and for the learners (refer to Chapter 8). This section is not just a restatement of work you did in previous chapters. During your field experience, your goals likely shifted as you realized more realistically what could and should be accomplished. Therefore, try to describe any modifications in goals and reasons for the changes, since, in part, the changes reflect your growth from the experience.

Learning

The heart of the report and of your field experience itself is what you learned from the experience. Just as your goals for yourself may have been multifaceted, so might your learning have been. For the purpose of this report, focus on what you learned about teaching. Although this focus limits the scope of the section on learning, there is still much room for diversity. What you learned about teaching might represent answers to one or more of the following questions:

1. What are the characteristics of an effective (successful or good) teacher? Answers to this question take the following form:
   Effective teachers are _____ (e.g., enthusiastic about their subject matter, caring, flexible, etc.).
2. What are the characteristics of an effective (successful, worthwhile, or good) lesson? Answer:
   Effective lessons are when _____ (e.g., children are actively involved).
3. What are crucial (or important) teaching skills? Answer:
   _____ (e.g., probing questions) is a crucial teaching skill.
4. What should teachers attempt to do or accomplish? Answer:
   Teachers should attempt to _____ (e.g., build self-confidence, set a good example, enter students' frame of reference, establish good rapport, emphasize the positive, gain respect of students, etc.).
5. What are important dilemmas that teachers face? Answer:
   An important dilemma that teachers face is _____ (e.g., whether to establish an informal or more formal teacher role; how to modify and direct teaching toward each student's need with 30 students in each class).

Questions 1, 2, and 4 address ideals of teaching. Question 3 obviously focuses on skills. Question 5 reflects unresolved issues that surface as a result of encountering problems.

Question 5 is the most open-ended, recognizing that field experience raises more issues than it resolves. This question draws directly on Chapters 6, 7, and 8. Question 1 draws directly on Chapter 10, and question 4 on Chapter 9.

These five questions do not exhaust the conclusions you might reach regarding teaching. Others include the needs of children (e.g., the need to be recognized), how children learn (e.g., learning is an active process), things of which teachers should be aware (e.g., different comprehension skills of children), and problems children face (e.g., identity crises). Whatever you did learn about teaching, make it explicit in your report.

Episodes

Presumably what you learned about teaching you learned from some episodes that occurred during your field experience. Typically these episodes represent either successes or failures that taught you something important. It is this aspect of your report that depends most heavily on your weekly logs (see Chapter 3). Logs provide case material, and this case material serves as illustrations of issues and evidence for conclusions you described in the preceding section on ideals, skills and dilemmas of teaching.

The two sections on "learning" and "episodes" are best treated as one integrated section. To interweave the two, you might proceed as follows:

1. Succinctly propose an ideal, skill, or dilemma of teaching. For example, dilemma: How much emphasis to place on real understanding or mastery of content while still covering all required topics.
2. Develop an argument for the importance of that particular ideal, skill, or dilemma, e.g., every time a teacher decides whether to entertain more student questions or terminate discussion of a topic, how quickly to pace a lecture, or how much emphasis to place on individual student project work, the teacher confronts the depth (i.e., mastery) versus breadth (i.e., coverage) dilemma.
3. Describe in detail from your logs one or two episodes that occurred that made you realize the importance of that particular ideal, skill, or dilemma.
4. Repeat 1, 2, and 3.

My students have found that between three and seven proposition-argument-episode items provide sufficient food for thought.

Generalizability

Since your report centers on what you learned from a *specific* situation, a brief discussion is helpful to address the generalizability of your conclusions. Would the same ideals, skills, or dilemmas apply to larger or smaller groups, to other subject matters, to different age students (and teachers), to students with special problems, and to other institutional, administrative, or societal contexts? This section, like the previous one, might be interwoven with the section on learnings, thus forming a set of learning-argument-episode-generalizability statements.

Goal Achievement

Reflecting back on your goals (see Chapters 2 and 8), try to assess the success you had in achieving those goals during your field experience.

If, like most people, you did not accomplish all you intended, consider the reasons for lack of goal achievement:

1. Unrealistic goals (e.g., not enough time)
2. Outside influences beyond your control (e.g., student's family)
3. Limitations in your own motivation or perseverance
4. Specific knowledge or skills you lacked
5. Specific traits you lacked
6. Your cooperating teacher
7. Your college supervisor
8. The principal

In the Appendix of this book are some progress reports written by students. Perhaps they will not only give you an idea of what a progress report looks like, but also inspire you to make the most of this opportunity to reflect on your field experience.

EPILOGUE

When I was a student in school, I could never understand why people called the end point of schooling "commencement." It was so confusing to me that I found myself using the word "commence" to mean "terminate." Of course, commencement referred to the beginning of life after school. What I realized much later is that we can consider the conclusion of any experience as a commencement, a period of getting ready for the next experience.

This book has focused on preparing for and reflecting on one particular experience. The conclusion of one particular experience is an opportune time for both reflection and preparation. It is a time to think back over one teaching experience and attempt to use it as a basis for planning the next experience.

Now might be a good time to make some plans for the future. While your field experience is still fresh in your mind, consider the following questions:

1. a. What issues have been raised by your field experience? Which ones remain unresolved?

   ▶

   b. What sorts of experiences do you think will enable you to work out some of these issues?

   ▶

2. a. What teaching skills do you need to work on?

   ▶

   b. How might you work on them?

   ▶

3. What kinds of teaching situations do you now need to try?

   ▶

4. What should you be doing in the meantime (for example, types of books to read, people to talk with, observations to make)?

   ▶

NOTES

1. Kevin Ryan et al., *Biting the Apple: Accounts of First-Year Teachers* (New York: Longman, 1980).
2. Raymond Corsini and Daniel Howard, *Critical Incidents in Teaching* (Englewood Cliffs, N.J.: Prentice-Hall, 1964).
3. Eliot Wigginton, *Sometimes a Shining Moment* (New York: Doubleday Books, 1987); Nancy Wallace, *Better Than School* (Burdett, N.Y.: Larson, 1983); Sylvia Ashton-Warner, *Teacher* (New York: Bantam Books, 1963); A. S. Neill, *Summerhill: A Radical Approach to Child Rearing* (New York: Hart, 1960).
4. Virginia Axline, *Dibs: In Search of Self* (Boston: Houghton Mifflin, 1964).

Appendix
Sample Progress Reports

SAMPLE PROGRESS REPORT 1

By Lori Hawley

The School for Special Children is a small, five-classroom school serving about 50 students from the surrounding five counties. Even though it is located in the country, the School is politically and financially city-oriented because of the bureaucratic and administrative ties to the city, county, state, and federal levels. *The Mission Statement,* however, is definitely oriented toward the child. An interdisciplinary team of therapists (speech, physical, and occupational), head teachers, and social workers work towards the overall development of each child's unique personality.

Sam, one of the cooperating teachers, is very responsive to the moods of the children in his room. He gives each of the children a chance to participate in a group activity on the rug in the back right corner of the room. Free play time is emphasized, and each of the children is encouraged to work at each of the three or four activities arranged on the tables, play "pretend" house in the house section, or play with the trucks or puppets from the large shelf off to the side.

Sharing and problem solving are also very important. The children are given certain responsibilities, e.g., feeding the guinea pig or watering the

---

Names of people, places, and schools have been changed in order to protect the privacy of those involved.

plants. Sam also believes in physical contact with the children and tries to give each child equal attention. Children who need extra help usually get it from the aides or volunteers. Sam also emphasizes creativity and allows the children to perform and make what they want without showing an elaborate model.

Another classroom is Sally's. Her classroom is larger than Sam's because it is divided into six Head Start children and six Special Children. The left near corner of the room is arranged to emphasize dramatic play, which Sally feels is quite important. Small groups of tables and shelves of toys are interspersed throughout the room. During the sharing time, half of the class gets to play that particular day. Some of the children do get upset by that, but most are used to it by now. These children are boisterous so there is more emphasis on trying to keep the children quiet during nap times than in Sam's room. Sally stresses communication and, thus, is quickly picking up the basics of sign language to talk with the hearing-impaired children. Sally is still finding her place but seems to be a strong teacher figure.

Goals

When I first began in January, I was idealistic and thought I would be given placement as a teacher/intern. Instead, since the teachers didn't know my background, they gave me observation and simple duties. Thus, my goals centered around learning new skills and changing certain habits/thoughts I had. Also, I wanted to develop my own style beyond the poor imitation I was performing (trying to do what the teachers did).

Now, after working with the children 16 hours per week for 14 weeks, I have realized that many of my skills I thought I needed to learn had already been formed. Although some of my beliefs did need changing, I worked on them all semester. One topic that kept reappearing was control/authority. Much of this stemmed from my need to feel equal with the other teachers. This led to a new goal: to see if I could really do it. I wanted to prove to the teachers and myself that I would make a good special education teacher. Once I was accepted and received more responsibility, I felt part of the team and loved it. I didn't realize how important it was to me, until one of the teachers said, "You've been here so long, I feel that you're a regular teacher." I felt so equal with those people, then.

My style changed, but not in the way I thought it would. It was not a mixture of Sam's and Sally's styles, but my own personality affected by their styles. But I surprised myself because I thought I would just be able to form my own style. But, in fact, I had a style all along—all I needed was the approval of others. Once out in the open, my style began to change of its own accord. In other words, I began to explore new possibilities and ways of teaching and learning from a project.

Learning

I've formed the opinion that an effective teacher is one who is caring and flexible. The person needs to understand the range of feelings others may feel and be willing to change his/her plans if they're not appropriate to the learners' capabilities on that particular day. (The teacher should be aware of the differences of comprehension skills of the children, as well). Thus, an effective lesson is when the children become actively involved in what the teacher is doing and are excited about it. I believe strongly that enthusiasm or at least piqued interest challenges the learner to make an effort to understand something and causes a higher degree of self-directed learning and motivation.

Other important aspects of education that can be considered are the teaching skills used. Examples of such crucial teaching skills are to have good communication with the learner, to make observations and interpretations of actions and problems, to have the ability to set realistic goals for the learner, and to measure progress reliably. These skills entail good listening and speaking abilities, the ability to observe and interpret the reactions to directions or remarks and then to form these observations into realistic goals that can be and should be reached.

The teacher should attempt to build self-confidence because so many of these children lose their motivation and feel inferior to others if they don't have a special proficiency of their own. Instead of losing interest and becoming careless about their work, they will care about others and feel that they aren't failures.

Some important dilemmas that teachers face are the authority/responsibility figures and the friend-teacher role. The authority/responsibility figure is the problem of understanding where to draw the line—how much do you do because you are responsible for the children (to a certain extent), and can you be an authority figure? This ties in with the teacher-friend role. If you're strictly a friend, can you suddenly turn authoritarian? Or do you become strictly teacher with no "friendly" background? Does a teacher have to connote an authority figure only at necessary times?

Of course, the children have needs and problems, too. They can become confused about the teacher if the teacher suddenly turns authoritarian. Another aspect that must be considered is how the children should learn. I believe it should be an active process in which they participate and direct some of their learning.

Episodes

An effective teacher is one who is caring and flexible, because children don't always have good days and teachers need to accept that. They need to have an alternative plan in case the first one doesn't seem too applicable.

Why? Because if the teacher is too inflexible, he/she may harm the learner's self-confidence, or relationship with the student. For example, when I worked with Alan and Doris in the gym, I acted too rigidly in making Doris move from the tarp. Because I felt that she shouldn't be the only one on the tarp, I didn't stop to think if there was an easier way to work it out. I just decided to take her off, which I did. Of course she became angry with me. But there was an alternative (which I didn't consider then)—to have had her share with Alan and Alan with her. Thus, I harmed my relationship with Doris and didn't express concern or recognize that her feelings were hurt.

Secondly, I believe that an effective lesson is one in which the children become actively involved in what the teacher is teaching; they become excited by it. I strongly believe that the children who become enthused are more willing to learn. Those who become active in the learning process learn the most. For instance, Alan learned quite a bit the day we worked with the colored sticks. And if he didn't master them all that day, he will learn them in the future because he will be willing to learn, based on his past happy experiences. I've never seen someone so excited about colors—especially when he got them right. He liked the mnemonic devices of "orange carrot," etc. and really tried the entire time we were working on them. His last statement says it all, "Aw, they turned off the lights. Now we'll have to put them away." He was truly disappointed that the interesting, happy learning experience had come to an end.

A third principle/skill that I suggested was having good communication with the learners. One example was shown in my third log. I stated:

> I caught myself wrongly communicating to the children. During playtime, the kids tried to walk on the grass. When I saw them go out there and when they asked me if they could go down the slide, I said, "No, Becky said to stay off the grass." (Becky had said no, but I forgot to adapt her saying to my own.) I neglected to say, "No, I don't want you to go out there, it's too wet."

Good communication is also attempting to talk on the child's level. Thus, I took a sign language class so that I could "talk" with Gary and Andy (hearing-impaired children). This helped very much, because Andy was scared of me in the first months. But now that I talk to him on his own level, he comes over to me, "chatters" on and on, and fights with others to sit on my lap during music!

For many teachers, observation and interpretation skills are needed. Why? Because the teacher has to be able to tell at a glance if a kid is missing, or interpret sounds into a thought, e.g., a teacher hears two children fighting and must be able to identify which kids were fighting and why they were fighting, and decide how to handle the situation. I didn't have to deal with many of these types of problems, but I had to sharpen these skills so that I could understand a little girl. I signed to Jill and she would sign back in a variated sign vocabulary. In other words, I have to watch intently to see what her answer is, because she doesn't always sign what she means or she copies my signs, or she gives such a stilted variation of the sign that I have problems interpreting the meaning. Interpretation comes in when I have to decide the meaning or "read" other aspects of Jill. For example, if she continually points to the side of the boat and raises her voice and signs "all done," I have a pretty good indicator that she wants to get out. But sometimes it's not so easy, and then I have to rely on how she has acted in the past. (Does she like to ride in the boat for ten minutes, or does she get tired after five minutes?) Thus, through experiences and careful observation, we can interpret what has happened or is happening in a situation. This can be critical if we see out of the corner of our eye a child hanging upside-down from the monkey bars and ten seconds later see him lying on the ground unconscious. We know what happened—he fell from the bars—and thus we won't have to waste time asking questions. Observation also helps in determining a child's behavior, for example, we can see that five out of seven times the child was attempting to count just as we had taught him.

Progress can be shown by illustrating the beginning performance, performances six weeks later, and then maybe twelve weeks later, and note the changes. It's useful for evaluation and helpful in noting if the goal will be met, if it can't be mastered, or if it needs to be altered. A good example of progress towards a goal is seen in Log No. 6, in which Jill showed considerable gain towards her physical therapist's stated goal: "to walk and turn without assistance." In January she had to be held by two hands to help her walk, but by early April she was able to be held for a forthcoming step and was able to "pick up her right foot and place it on the mat and then place the other on it. We walked across the mat, but then had to turn around so we wouldn't get hit by the swing. I told her what we had to do and I moved the ball slowly in a circle. She held on the whole time and moved her left foot to the left side and then the right followed (she didn't fall once). She helped direct the ball and was very excited when she walked across the mat to the floor; she stepped down without hesitation or jolt." Now, a month later, she walks erect with no help or support and gets better and better every day. That's progress!

The teacher should also try to build up self-confidence, because she can really make the child feel important or inferior if the child doesn't have a specialty or knows the teacher thinks he or she is a "dumb" child. How does a teacher foster self-confidence? By praising the child when he does well, showing a child's work to the rest of the class, or asking a child's advice. Let's use Jill again for an example. When she finished a complete turn and walked all around without falling, I really praised her and told everyone what she had done. Once she saw that she could walk by herself, she kept practicing until she was able to go on her own. Thus, the warm praise gave her motivation for more praise and so she walked without aid. The more confidence she gained, the more she kept pushing herself. And she did it!

Last, a big dilemma faced by many interns and student teachers is the question of authority and how it relates to the teacher–friend role. My opinion is that the teacher needs to integrate the friend and teacher roles as totally as possible. When a control problem comes up, the teacher side should be more forceful but rely on the friend–friend relationships to rectify the problem. As a beginning teacher, I discovered that I had to be a friend first and foremost, because I didn't have a relationship on which to base my authority. For example, in Log No. 1, I played with Gary to keep him quiet and on his cot, because I didn't have the "right" to yell at him and say, "It's time to sleep now!" I was still working out our relationship. In Log No. 4, though, I did use my teacher authority to get James to go over the tooth-brushing area. But unfortunately, I don't believe I based it on our friendship, but that I felt my authority was being tested. But by Log No. 7, I had realized that my role did not have to be forceful. I could let the children work out their problems and only intervene when necessary. Also, instead I stressed, "I had to remove you, Chris, because you broke the rules. You know you are not supposed to throw sand." Chris, by this time, regarded me as one of his teachers and obeyed my directions to leave the sandbox without a fuss.

Generalizability

Most of my ideals, dilemmas, and skills would apply to any group, large or small, to different subjects, to different age groups or students from different backgrounds. Learners from any of these groups would want to have self-confidence, have fun while learning, have a caring teacher who understood the teacher–friend role and communicated effectively. Also, I'm quite sure they would appreciate someone who had good observation and interpretation skills so that the progress would be accurately determined.

Goal Attainment

Most of my goals were sufficiently achieved as far as I had anticipated. My style has developed on its own without much thought until the last work session with Alan. I suddenly realized I wasn't copying Sally or Sam anymore and was even using different techniques for myself. I ended up even further than I expected.

Overall, I loved my placement. I had a shaky start, but once I became used to this unique school system and had established relationships with the children and staff, I realized I had much to offer. I feel that I have progressed to the point that I can say, "I am a special education teacher," and I love the thought of it!

SAMPLE PROGRESS REPORT 2

BY JOHN LANGAN

One would have trouble disputing that the community within which my field experience took place is, in terms of geography, ethnicity, and socio-economic status, a very diverse one. There is about the same "white" and "black" proportion as in most other small northeastern U.S. cities. The overwhelming presence of a college, however, adds cultural groups from all parts of the world. The city is fairly isolated from other urban areas, so that there is a large rural student component in the schools.

If one wished to cut through the diversity, though, and generalize (as I will here), most students fall into one of two broad categories: those whose parents are involved in the educational system (vocationally), and those whose parents aren't. The teachers face a clash of varying expectations from the two parental groups. The former group seems to opt for a highly intellectual, competitive school environment, "so our kids can get used to what the real world is like and, hopefully, come out on top." The latter group tends to hope for a more practical, caring, cooperative academic environment so their kids don't get left behind and so they get the academic assistance which they themselves may be unable to provide.

"Isolated" would be the proper adjective to describe the setting of the Middle School. Four lanes of highway converge with the steep slopes of a nearby hill to provide a "moat" which makes escape highly unlikely.

"Where are you supposed to be?!" is the most oft-heard phrase in the halls during class time. The highly social, silly situation in the library makes it almost impossible for the serious student to concentrate.

The walls are, for the most part, barren, except for a few teacher-designed displays of role models (black scientists, famous women, and high tech geological, engineering displays) with the message: "School may seem unrewarding, but look what could happen to you if you apply yourself."

The classroom is stuffy and hot with completely artificial lighting—a room not meant for science use and not compensated for by the district with any experimental materials. "Just *expose* them to the materials, Bill," the head of the science department said, "they'll have plenty of experiments to do in the next few years." The room is always crowded, with 30 students. Many are normally high-strung, anxious, and even violent; others internal.

A very few appear confident and at peace with themselves. Being sixth graders (11–13 years old), the range of physical, emotional, and cognitive development is extremely broad.

Bill is a certified high school history teacher. He has no trouble running a science class because he is anxious to learn, fair, caring, enthusiastic, well-respected, humorous, and interesting—an excellent role model and cooperating teacher. He admits that unfortunately he does see himself as teaching a "class" and not a group of individuals. "There's just too many of them!" He seems to gear material to those most academically developed, hoping that the less-developed kids will at least get enough out of each subject to keep up. It is more fun and challenging for him to teach the more difficult material, and his greatest fear is "boring someone, or holding them back."

I arrived in late October as a "teacher's aide." My goals initially were very vague. I wanted to find out what teaching was really like; I wanted to see if I could express well to others what I have learned myself; and I hoped to be able to be both friend and instructor to the students.

Bill and I were discussing each other's expectations, and I formed another situational goal. Since this was only his second year teaching science, with no previous background, there were many areas where he could really use my input. My goal was to complement the education students would have gotten with just Bill alone by teaching the subjects he felt least strong in.

As the year passed, however, it became apparent that I lacked the time and energy to devote to learning material and preparing lectures, materials, handouts, etc. So, since at that point the many problems of large class situations were clear to me, I altered my goal from its original intent of being another Bill with different material. I was determined instead to provide individual attention to those most needy. I was eager to do this by providing direct experiences with nature and by bringing "success" to students with obvious inferiority complexes.

Ideal

We must instill a sense of success in each child's head to promote development of a good self-concept. A good self-concept is a prerequisite for initiative and curiosity in learning.

The *3 Rs* are given such great emphasis in elementary school and the individual's performance in these subjects is so closely observed and so quickly judged by society, that it is no surprise to me that many youngsters base their self-concept primarily upon this performance. By this reasoning, a student who, for whatever reason, begins his career in these subjects picking things up at a slower rate (with greater difficulty) than most of his peers will see himself as a failure. So soon! As with many other aspects of humanity, we have the unfortunate tendency to imagine one's learning capacity to be fixed, to remain static even with the continually changing circumstances of life. So the student whose first couple of years of academia have not been "successful" may have dug a hole for himself, perhaps setting the tone for a lifetime of low self-esteem.

I witness many sixth-grade students deeply embedded in that hole. Interestingly, I find a common thread which links them. They each enjoy and excel at an activity not recognized by the school as deserving of status. Can we not, as teachers, help instill the idea to all members of the class that *any* activity in life can be a learning experience, that each of us has something educational to offer to another? We can all pool our various strengths together to help each individual become a stronger whole. Instead, students are encouraged to pull away from each other (to look down with pride, or upward with envy) in the competition for success in the *3 Rs*.

I think teachers should look more closely at what preoccupies the minds of those individuals who seem "to be going nowhere." When we understand their favored activity, we must inform the child that success in that effort can be as important as success in any other endeavor. Let the child share his success with others and urge others to respect and learn from it.

If, and this is my main point here, we can somehow expand what the word "school" means to an elementary student, then students who excel at activities other than the *3 Rs* could increase their self-esteem in school. Higher self-esteem should open these students up to new strength, less fear of failure, and more initiative and curiosity to learn the *3 Rs*. Vice versa, those who excel at the *3 Rs*, but who never felt they could be successful at other activities, might give them a try.

I understand that the most important skills needed to keep society functioning are the *3 Rs*. However, we cannot blindly push these skills and place all other activities of life in a background position. My feeling is that overall societal proficiency in the *3 Rs* would increase if there were also other important curricular activities to succeed at.

Bryan was presented to me as a student in dire need of math help. "I know he can do the problems," Bill said, "He just doesn't concentrate or line them up right, so he screws up in the semantics of problem solving and is excruciatingly slow." Ditto in science class, where his interest is much higher but his notebook is the biggest mess of crumpled sheets you've ever seen. He is so spacy, uninterested for the most part in conventional curricula. But he's always telling me stories, eyes lit up with confident savvy, about tracking animals, bow hunting, climbing trees, building forts, fishing, making bird houses, and assorted other adventures. Bryan is very advanced in his knowledge about nature, but he sees himself, based on his grades in the *3 Rs*, as stupid—a failure.

He, and a few other kids from rural areas (essentially in the same academic strangles as Bryan), got me thinking about making nature a larger part of the curriculum. This topic was particularly appropriate, being my area of "expertise." I started a series of Tuesday nature hikes in a nearby park. Part of the Thursday science classes is devoted to the kids' reporting their findings to the rest of the class. Bryan was on the first trip. He dressed for school that day in a coonskin cap and rawhide vest. He got everyone excited about nature, both in school and in the woods (where his natural curiosity uncovered three or four times as many items of interest as anyone else). His demonstration and fielding of questions were done with great flair and confidence. He accompanied his findings as they were passed around the room to explain them to each individual.

Since that week Bryan has presented himself with much more esteem, even haughtiness. His schoolwork in the *3 Rs* has greatly improved, seriously. Somehow I think he's had a chance to step back and say, "Well, it's not fun, but I gotta do it, and I'm strong enough to give it my best." Maybe it's hard to have your self-concept improved and still devote so little energy to the necessary topics of life.

When Mark is sent back to me for help in science, he reaches a moment when something becomes difficult to him; then he jumps up from his seat, performs a couple of graceful, yet spasmodic, break-dancing moves, and then sits back down smiling. He's happy, but he says he can't do the work in school, he hates it. Music is on Mark's mind. I got the idea that we could make Mark see his dancing as part of his school experience. Bill, laughing, gave me permission to use one class period a week to give Mark a break-dancing seminar. Now I can't even do the box step, but Mark and I entered the gym with a "ghetto-blaster," and Grandmaster "Flash" and Herbie Hancock tapes. He went wild for about an hour. I scrutinized his moves, whistle in mouth, pointing out edges in need of smoothing! Here's an educational twist. In the three sessions so far, we have discussed fractions and physics during break-dancing. He had to come in on the third beat of the total four in the sequence (so 4 was a whole and 3/4, etc.). He seemed to grasp fractions for the first time. It hit home—fractions in music?! Maybe fractions are cool to know. The physics learning came when he was spinning on the floor, and he wanted to know why he spun faster when he pulled his legs in. Within the realm of every activity, many others can be taught!

Two weeks ago, Mark performed solo in the center of class for five minutes. People shouted "All right, Mark!" I don't think he received praise that much before. He gave everybody "five" and sat down beaming. He feels good lately. "I wanta be a professional dancer." He was waiting for my look; it was a joke between us. Then he added, smiling, "Oh, yeah . . . after I finish this school stuff."

This method of bringing "success" to a child's feeling of school will be most far reaching and beneficial if done as early in the child's school career as possible, and if done on an individual basis. However, in any stage of the life cycle and in all administrative, institutional, or societal contexts, we can all use some "success."

Dilemma

How much attention to place on the social-emotional needs of children, while still giving enough emphasis to academic skill development?

Time spent within the walls of the school is a large chunk of a sixth grader's life. My feeling, however, is that many sixth graders see academia as a secondary aspect of living. Everyone has a few emotional problems and bouts with unhappiness. Fortunately, most of these sixth graders are lucky enough to have already erected ego mechanisms so that they can stabilize themselves for the tasks at hand during school, putting aside their problems. To use a metaphor, their emotional problems are like a spring shower in the mind. Using an umbrella, they can easily shield the rain, and function with little effort. Some students' minds, however, are tumultuous with emotional disarray, whether due to academics itself, social interactions, or external situations. They have a regular hurricane in the mind; a flimsy umbrella would break in pieces upon immediate exposure. For these students it's problematic for teachers to attempt erecting new knowledge in the midst of such a storm.

To oversimplify, for these students to learn, we must help diminish the storm so their minds can concentrate on other activities such as learning. There is, to me, no way of getting around paying attention to the social-emotional needs of certain kids. Otherwise, even if the child grabs a few of the academic skills you are tossing out, eventually they will be buried with the storm, destroyed, not to be built upon or connected with other skills.

My task one morning was to "assist" Ernie with his math. Just from his files, one can picture a child with many emotional problems. His father is an unemployed alcoholic who has attempted suicide three times in the past year. His mother has been described as very meek and mildly "retarded," unloving to Ernie because she's looking for love and security herself. Being an only child and living 10 miles out of town (the next neighbor is one half mile away), Ernie doesn't get much chance to play or talk with anyone. He is internalized and, to apply my metaphor, there's a storm in there. He thinks he's stupid, and it's obvious he's always been led to believe that. He's never really mastered his times tables even though he's been exposed to them since third grade. I believe his emotional-social problems were the initial cause of his math problems. But when he didn't pick it up with the rest of the class, he was tracked in the lowest math level, another piece of evidence in his mind that he is stupid. Whenever someone now tries to help him, he feigns complete disinterest to cover up for lack of knowledge. He doesn't want another person to think he's stupid. It builds and builds. He has to protect himself.

So this day I decided to forget math goals and let him air his restless mind. I asked him what he did last night, what television shows he watched, etc. His first words were blurted out, "I gotta worry about walking home this afternoon." He said he was kicked off the bus today for fighting, and his family had no car. Would you have been able to do math if you were in his predicament?! I reassured him I would drive him home. He looked astonished and pleased.

Then he looked at me and sighed, "You're weird, John," but I think he meant I was different when I talked to him like an individual. I was called to the front by Bill to pass out homework. When I came back in about five minutes, I was amazed to see that Ernie had completed all but two problems on the sheet. He didn't expect a pat on the back for this quick spurt of work. He just said, "I hate math." The bell rang and he left without his bookbag and gloves. I had released some of the storm, but really only a local squall. Much more abatement at the core is necessary for real, continual learning.

Solving this dilemma requires that we do treat the classroom as a group of individual personalities with varying needs, each of which deserves to be addressed. This dilemma is most often encountered during the period of development before strong ego formation and thus is not completely generalizable to older students. But there are points in everyone's life where emotional stress inhibits performance in societal tasks.

Ideal

A maximum of direct experience with subject matter should be provided.

Most classroom lessons in the sixth grade are designed so that children utilize only one of their senses (hearing) and at most two (add vision). When providing direct experience with an object or phenomenon, we should stress using all the senses to form the fullest sensual image possible. The student is led to discover for himself those ideas that before had only been talked about or diagrammed on boards and transparencies. He forms his own unique sensual image from the experience, an image more shocking, more liable to be lodged into memory, fuller, more real, more provocative of further investigation.

Experiential learning also provides a chance for student and teacher to learn together, feel more equal, and become closer by sharing a common excitement. Direct experience can also help revive the energy of students who are having trouble devoting concentration and interest to a curriculum they feel just doesn't relate to their everyday life. Learning becomes more tangible and can be fun to repeat and expand outside school in everyday situations.

One day during our unit on human biology, the parents of a student arrived with a bag of goodies. They unloaded onto a table two respiratory systems (pig and cow), two hearts, a cow's leg, a sheep's calf and hoof, and a cow skull with eye and brain. Students arrived with looks and shouts of "eww," held noses, and cast away eyes, or else they looked like, "Ah, this doesn't bother me, you sissies, c'mon let's be mature." We offered sanctuary in the library for those too squeamish. No one left. Kids inflated lungs and watched them get light, airy, and ten times as large. The "eww" changed to "wow!" Everybody got excited feeling lubrication fluid in joints, opening heart valves, checking out the optic nerve, pulling tendons to make the hoof open and close, smelling, etc. They'll never forget it. The room was filled between periods with other curious onlookers. The most unlikely candidates were proudly announcing futures as doctors and vets.

Another time I gave a lecture on flowers and pollination. It went well. However, had the second part of the lesson not been a flower dissection, I'm sure the whole concept would not have crystallized half as well. (A test two weeks later showed great overall comprehension.) Most of the students had never seen how interesting, complex, functional, and beautiful the inners of a flower are. They took it apart, looked at pollen and ovules under a magnifying glass, plucked off a stamen, and pollinated the stigma of other people's flowers. They tasted nectar and smelled its perfume. The bug-eyes and ample questions indicated they no longer thought of flowers as just pretty ornaments.

The last part of the year, every Tuesday I have led a group of six students on nature walks in a nearby park. I saw two general ways that a nature walk could enhance the education process; it could initiate and enlighten the never before exposed; and it could show those already "nature-kids" that, yes, knowledge in this area is appreciated and important. The latter group happens to be made up largely of students having trouble in the *3 Rs*. They would use a chance to prove they're good at something, and to be shown that school can relate to their everyday practical life experiences.

When on the trip you can explain concepts, but not too many. Allow for ample exploration and discovery. Urge smelling, touching, tasting—using all the senses to register in your mind this experience. Don't point everything out! If he finds it himself, the experience will be much more memorable and powerful. If someone approaches you excited with a find, but you have no idea what it is, do not hedge! No, rather, embrace the opportunity to learn and be excited together. Admit your ignorance, but engage in the same natural curiosity the student is feeling. The student may feel the relationship become closer, more human.

This ideal is universally generalizable. There's no substitute for the real thing!

Dilemma

Students at the top of the class academically have learned to play it safe. For them to develop, they must be aided in taking risks, sailing uncharted seas, and opening up their mind's insight, intuition, and imagination again.

It seems as though from the first to fifth grade, children are drilled in the *3 Rs* to such an extent that their natural curiosity and imaginations have been pounded into subservience to the processes of memorization and dualistic reasoning. Their minds will accept only what is first explicitly stated by the teacher. Every question must have a right and wrong answer. When providing a new angle to an issue, they yell, "But you said before to do it this way!" Perhaps one of the most difficult tasks of the sixth-grade teacher is to teach an understanding of the many approaches to most issues and problems, relativistic reasoning, and forming one's own views.

For the future of our society, it is very important for people to be educated to the fact that many issues simply cannot be broken down into an exact right and wrong position. There is complexity inherent in almost every situation, and this must be stressed. The biggest danger in forming one's view is the possibility of misconceptions, misinterpretations, and bias. Therefore, undistorted reasoning and open-mindedness must be taught and urged. No longer should students accept as complete truth the views of their teachers or books, nor should they be rewarded for simply rehashing these views. They must learn to reason through the issues by themselves.

The entire sixth grade was to embark on their first real research paper. The teachers wanted students to gain the necessary knowledge about term paper structure and style and were much less concerned with content. Four very bright (academically) girls had previously (last year) been led by their fifth-grade teacher through the basics of notetaking, outlines, contents, bibliography, etc. We did not want them to be subject to this same material again. I was to have each Tuesday and Thursday to challenge them to produce a paper in which thought, work, and content took the forefront.

At first they basked in the prestige of the select honor. Then the next week, with frustrated looks, they spoke to me of not having done much at all. "Everyone else has such a firm idea of what type of information to look for," they moaned; "we didn't know what we were supposed to find out."

"We're not having fun."

"Why, I mean this stuff is interesting," I said.

"But we don't know what a lot of it means."

"It's no fun because it's not easy?" I asked.

No one spoke. I think I hit it on the head. They wanted to do what everyone else was doing because it would bring them an A without much work (or thought) at all. In that paper there would be certain things which could be marked wrong with an "X". It was offering them the chance to form their own impression of right or wrong, and it overwhelmed them. But that's understandable, considering that until this point their written work had, for the most part, been mere reiteration of memorized ideas. For this paper they needed to form relationships from ideas, to use inductive reasoning. It was too much to expect them to cross this wide gap alone.

I calmed them and we talked about "opinions." I told them they all had opinions on many issues. I began to discuss abortion. The discussion became heated, and they all offered many good points.

"Now, does anyone have the completely right answer to the abortion issue!"

They understood.

"But you all have viewpoints, and you could write them down."

The point came out that, yeah, they had opinions, but not ones which could be trusted compared to the teacher's. They felt that the closer their opinion came to matching that of the teacher, the more he would like their paper. Hmm. It bothered me that there might be truth to that statement. I dispelled this notion for my case by stating that I wanted most to see papers where you could see the development of the best viewpoint they could muster, based on the information which I would help provide.

"Relax. For once don't worry about grades, worry about learning," I pleaded. "What will please me most is that you try to learn."

This dilemma is especially prevalent at around sixth grade, because of the history of their education and cognitive development up to that stage. Early adolescence is the time of the beginnings of inner identity development, formal operations, and relativistic thinking.

However, it is generalizable in the sense that many people lapse into the security of "playing it safe," closing their minds (its curiosity and imagination), and taking fewer risks (on the job, economically, socially).

I have had so much "food for thought" stemming from my field experience. With reflection, it becomes clear that there is always something new to learn about teaching. We do our best, but the more you increase the resolution of the macroscope and look at your class, rough edges and impurities that you never thought about become visible. In this sense, goal number one can never be completely fulfilled, by anyone. You can never know exactly what teaching is really like. The more you see, the less you know.

More practically, as a student teacher, the entire class is never, in a realistic sense, "yours." So it would be impossible anyway to find out what teaching a sixth-grade class is like. I gained much insight and exposure, however, to what it is like to teach individuals or small groups.

Because it was not my role to lay down class rules, and because it was hard to understand my degree of authority, students questioned my status as "one deserving that respect we give when we don't want to get into trouble." That being the case, it was difficult to find the fine line between friendship and authority.

My final goals were: providing attention for individuals who were most needy; offering direct communion with nature; and bringing "success" to students with inferiority complexes. Action on my part was all that was necessary to fulfill these goals, and I acted. I only wish I could have reached more people and had more time to spend.

I see myself, years hence, repeating that last sentence as I lie dying.

SAMPLE PROGRESS REPORT 3

By Robin Katz

Driving down to Cedarcrest Elementary School at 9 o'clock on a Friday morning to teach art, I think about the community. The steep hill of Maple Street where Central School is located is lined with quaint colonial and Victorian houses, each one distinctly designed and landscaped. These unique houses reflect the many individuals of the community, for they are as varied as the community's diverse inhabitants. The many nature lovers enjoy the breathtaking views from the surrounding hills and the beautiful foliage. The "artsies" frequent the Wolcott Museum and attend the many plays and the music and dance performances constantly going on in town. The professionals and "yuppies" provide law services and medical needs and run the banks and the many businesses in town. Finally, the intellectuals, the students, and the professors at the local colleges spend their time researching and learning. What binds all of these diverse people together is their overall support and pride in the colleges as well as their support of education in general.

I turn in on North Street by the school and park my car. Through the door leading to the playground, I enter the school into a hallway brightly decorated with displays of students' work. Coat hooks and little cubbies with name tags also line the corridor. As I walk towards the art room, I hear phrases from lessons and bits of chatter. It is a happy atmosphere.

A three-foot-high wall creates an aisle leading to the main interior of the art room. Windows with hanging plants let natural light shine over the aisle, into the room. There are a stove and a sink at the back of the room and two fish tanks filled with colorful fish. Materials such as scissors, crayons, and construction paper are neatly labeled and stacked in boxes and crates along two walls of the room. Above the back area is a loft where no more than six children at a time can play. In the loft are two tables and chairs, a huge bean bag, and a ''junk box'' of scrap materials and odds and ends with which children make creative crafts. There is a sign that reads, ''No weapons. You make 'em, we take 'em,'' hanging in front of the loft. In the middle of the room are two long picnic tables with benches and two smaller tables with chairs. Decorative lights add to the room's brightness from the colorful student art work hanging along the walls. Everything about the room says art, even the slight scent of glue, magic markers, and tempera paint. This cheery place is quite conducive to art!

Fran Stiles, my cooperating teacher, is one of the most positive aspects of this art room since she is the woman who set up this creative environment. Before the children file in for each art class, Fran always has the materials for the lesson spread out across the tables. Once the students sit along the table, Fran explains what they will be making during the period and demonstrates how to use the materials to make the project. Everyone works on his (or her) project until five minutes before the period ends in order to clean up. Then either the class's next teacher will come to get them or Fran will escort the children to their next class and bring back the next group she will be working with.

Fran's students respect her as their art teacher but also consider her a friend. As the childen work on their projects, Fran often talks with them about mutual interests and current events in her or their lives. She cares about art and her students, and her students care in return.

The warm atmosphere was the setting for my field experience. When I first began, I was immediately thrown into class. Before the students arrived, Fran and I talked briefly and she explained the lesson plan to me. Once the children came in, she introduced me as someone who would be helping out during the semester. She demonstrated the lesson, then had the children start working. She told me to jump right in. Feeling lost and confused, I sat down at one of the big tables, took a deep breath, and forced myself to immediately become a part of that class. I talked with the children and helped them when they needed it. By the end of class I had talked a little bit with each of the twenty students about their projects. I had made a difference in that class.

It was not until after that first class that I seriously thought about my goals: the ''differences'' I wanted to make. For myself, I wanted to experience teaching art firsthand, since I have been considering it as a possible career. Being a fine arts major, I have spent many hours observing and participating in art education, but I have mostly been on the receiving end of learning—other than helping a few classmates with problems. The only structured teaching experience I had was in offering a period in T-shirt painting once a week at a day camp where I worked for six weeks. Yes, I was in charge of all aspects involved in running the lesson, but I wanted to experience teaching in a scholastic environment. I also wanted to see how well I would fare as a teacher. Being a student, I feel I am very attuned to other students' needs and wishes. I can easily recognize an unclear explanation and know what an awful feeling it is to be lost and unsure of myself in a class. Also, I enjoy reexplaining concepts and procedures to friends. I know what I expect to get out of a lesson and have a good idea as to what others expect too, so I thought it would be fun and interesting to reverse roles and see how well I would do as a teacher. In addition, I wanted to pass on my knowledge and love for art. Art plays a major role in our lives and helps to beautify society. Art is a decoration, communication, emotion, fashion, and more. Without it, our lives would be less colorful—in all aspects of the word! It is important to me, then, that I pass on an appreciation for art and hopefully inspire creativity in my students and help to teach them the basic tools of the craft.

I believe Fran shares this last goal of wanting to pass on an appreciation and knowledge of art, for this seems the basis for wanting to teach any subject of personal importance. My all-encompassing goal for my students is also applicable to all learned subjects and is the thread that binds my subordinate goals specific to art. This major goal I wanted my students to achieve is one of self-direction. Even in my own studies I have found that self-direction leads to achievement and success. For example, I will never forget an awful algebra teacher I had in eleventh grade, for taking his course taught me the value of self-direction. His teaching was so poor that what I got out of his class was the ability to teach myself. I was forced to take the initiative to learn the material from the text in order to do well in his course. Taking the initiative is the key to self-direction, for it involves motivation, creative thinking, and confidence, and finally leads to self-fulfillment of knowledge. Learning through initiative is the best type of learning, for when students take active roles in their education, they will better understand and remember what they have learned; they will have chosen to care about their education and their intellectual growth.

It was not until the end of my field experience, as I looked back on my logs, that I realized this overall goal of self-direction that I had hoped for my students to achieve. As I read through the many episodes that occurred, I thought about how much I enjoyed teaching art at Cedarcrest Elementary School, even though it was not always easy. In fact, I found I was challenged most when things did not run smoothly. And from three specific dilemmas that occurred, I realized three individual goals underlying the goal of self-direction that I wanted my students to achieve in order to overcome their problems. To overcome the problem of the students' wanting too much help from me, I wanted to inspire them to be self motivated. In dealing with a lack of ideas, I wanted to inspire my students to think creatively.

Finally, the fear of making mistakes was a dilemma best overcome by building students' confidence.

Each of the three dilemmas that I faced presented me with a problem for which I tried to find a quick solution, and these solutions were based on the goals I wanted my students to achieve. The dilemmas forced me not to act as I would have in more general situations but to evaluate quickly the problem and *re*act specifically to them. The first dilemma I mentioned was that all too often the children wanted me to practically do their work for them. This problem is apparent not only in art but in all areas of teaching, and it stems from a lack of motivation. Students know that having the teacher do the work for them is the easiest way out. Yet little learning takes place in such situations. Laziness and a "who cares?" attitude cause the dilemma.

In art, the problem is that students often want the teacher to make all the creative decisions and perhaps even go as far as to do the work for them. This dilemma occurred in the very first class I taught at the school. Fran had the children working on pop-out cards that they were to design, using crayons or magic markers. Some of the students went right to work drawing on their cards, but many others came up to me and asked if I would do drawings for them. At first I was glad to draw for them because I thought it would be a good way to become quickly a useful member of the class and to make the children like me. Besides, it was easier for me, too, to draw for them and please them rather than refuse to draw and upset them; this is the reason why many teachers fall into the trap of doing the students' work—it is often convenient for the teachers as well as for the students. But after a while, I realized that it was their art class, not mine, and that my doing their drawings was not helping them learn about art. I wanted them to walk out of class holding cards they had drawn themselves. At this point I realized one of my goals was to get these children excited about art and to inspire motivation so that they would want to do their own work. Motivation, then, is one of the factors of self-direction, which will lead to productive results!

My solution was based on the desire to motivate the students. One girl in particular asked me to draw her a cat. Instead of flatly refusing to do so, I asked her to describe verbally what a cat looked like; she felt more comfortable talking about it than drawing it on paper. Since there were no cats or reproductions of cats in the room, I could not help her with hand-eye coordination, but I could help her to draw from her memory and imagination. As she described a cat, I handed her an unintimidating scrap piece of paper and asked her to show me what a cat looks like, too. The next thing she knew, her drawing of a cat was sitting in front of her. She was so excited that she proceeded to draw an even better cat on her pop-out card.

With a little push from me, she was motivated to draw on her own and took pride in her finished product.

Another dilemma I faced was the students' lack of ideas. Often, Fran assigned projects that were material-specific but not product-specific, such as finger puppets and Valentine's Day cards, in which the children had to use papier-mâché and various construction papers, but their manner of decoration was completely up to them to design. I cannot count how many times over the course of my field experience I heard, "I don't know what to draw." I can relate to this dilemma, for in my own experiences I have often found it difficult to come up with good ideas for my art work. It is fun to work with a good idea since it can stand up on its own even if it is not shown in its best light, but a bad idea, no matter how well executed, will always be bad. Besides, with a mediocre idea a student will work only for an exterior motive as for a grade, rather than work self-directed. The solution for this dilemma is based on creative thinking, or problem solving.

In art, every project is a new challenge in which students must design in order to produce inventive results. My goal for them was to help inspire creative thinking in order to overcome this dilemma, and I had the opportunity to do so in a particular class. Fran gave the children a project to design T-shirts to be used possibly for the town's annual festival coming up this spring. One group of boys sitting at the far end of a picnic table seemed to have trouble with this, though. The assignment sounded simple enough, but these boys were having problems thinking of important or interesting aspects of the town festival that they could draw. Instead, many boys were drawing cartoon characters from Saturday morning television shows, which had nothing to do with the festival. I sat down next to this group of boys and asked them what they were drawing; they showed me their pictures of "Astrodog" flying in space. When I asked them about the festival theme, they shrugged. Only a few had actually gone to the festival before, so I could understand their difficulty in coming up with ideas. To get their creative juices flowing, I played an association game with them. I asked the boys who had been to the festival to tell the others what they remembered about it; then I told all of the boys that the festival was similar to a carnival and asked those who had gone to carnivals to describe what they remembered about them. Objects associated with festivals and carnivals started coming up in discussion, and when one mentioned one aspect of a carnival, such as brightly colored balloons, this sparked an idea in another boy, who mentioned fun games and rides. One particular boy, Patrick, thought of the location where the festival is held every spring—down on Main Street—and that is what he finally drew for his T-shirt design. Through group discussion and association, Patrick, as well as the others, came up with creative ideas, which they executed well on paper. So creative thinking leads to well-designed logos and is another step towards self-direction.

Since art often requires talent, many children lacked confidence in their abilities and often made mistakes. Lack of confidence is often a self-fulfilling prophecy, for if students do not feel they are capable of completing projects successfully, then chances are good that they will not. Also, it is unfortunate that at a young age society had instilled in us the belief that if you are going to do something, then do it right or don't do it at all. Such perfectionism is enough to drive a student crazy and make him fear making mistakes. Yet making mistakes is a major part of one's learning experience, for if you spend a lot of time doing something incorrectly, once you realize you are wrong, you will go out of your way to avoid making the same mistake in the future. Mistakes are often the hardest lessons to learn but are also the best remembered lessons.

During one of my own lessons I taught six students how to make pom-pom creatures from yarn and other materials. A small girl had trouble cutting her yarn evenly, so when she tied her strands together, the result looked more like a scraggly tassel than a pom-pom. I noticed her disappointment as she told me hers had come out wrong. I helped her by suggesting she work with her mistake by making it into what I suddenly named a "shaggy" instead of a pom-pom. Rather than fluffing out the yarn to make a round pom-pom, I pushed the yarn down in one direction to make it look like a tassel. Pleased, she decorated it and made what I thought was the best creature out of the six student creations. A boy also deviated from the original pom-pom idea once he saw this girl doing so. He was having trouble making an evenly round pom-pom, too, and was glad to have the opportunity to alter his original plans to make a more interesting creature by decorating it as a double tassel.

In a small way, my helping these students work with their mistakes taught them that things do not always go the way you hope they will, so you should make the best of a situation. Just because a project is not turning out exactly like a preconceived notion doesn't mean it is necessarily turning out wrong. My goal was to get my students to be daring enough to be innovative and "go with the flow." They should not fear mistakes but rather feel challenged by them and attack them in order to make something good and perhaps even better than if their work had gone as planned. The small girl and boy proved to themselves that they could do just that, which, in turn, built up their confidence.

As I look back on my field experience, I feel as if I have achieved my personal goals as well as those directed towards my students. In addition to observing a teacher I respected and liked, I also had many opportunities to experience teaching firsthand and to test my own abilities. I enjoyed teaching art at the school and feel that I really did make a difference working with the kindergarten and first-grade classes. Although I never led any philosophical discussions about the value of art, I think my love of art showed through in my enthusiasm as I taught, and it rubbed off on my students: so many of them at the end of class left the art room smiling as they proudly clutched their works of art. Fran had much to do with this! What a rewarding feeling for me, though, when one girl came up to me and told me she always makes pom-pom creatures at home. In addition, I feel I succeeded in inspiring motivation, promoting creative thinking, and building confidence in the students, for they built upon what I taught them from lesson to lesson. By the end of my field experience, they knew that I expected them to turn to their own resources to accomplish great projects, and they did. The students still have a way to go, but I think I have helped to put them on their way towards self-direction.

SAMPLE PROGRESS REPORT 4

By Amy Tietjen

Girl Scout Troop #3 was not the first Girl Scout troop I had ever worked with. I had been a Girl Scout for seven years, I worked with a Brownie troop when I was a Girl Guide, and I was a counselor at a Girl Scout camp one summer. Although I know every group is different, I was not really prepared for the dissension that arose while I was working with this one.

The troop consisted of 13 girls: 9 fourth graders and 4 fifth graders. We met once a week after school in a classroom at the Elm Street Elementary School, and we just recently spent a weekend camping together. I worked with two co-leaders. The first, Judy Malloy, is a fourth-grade teacher (she has four of the Scouts in her class), and she is the mother of one of the girls. The second, Lynn Warren, is a woman who has no children and decided to work with the troop in order to spend some time with children and find out how she relates to them. Her other reason for deciding to work with Girl Scouts was the same as mine: we had both been Girl Scouts ourselves and had gotten so much from the experience that we wanted to share what we had experienced with another troop.

So my original goal was to have these girls do a lot of the same activities that I had done with other troops that I had been in and worked with and, hopefully, to get as much out of it as I had. This included songs, games, crafts, camping, and working on badges. Also, all of the troops that I had worked with were overseas. They had been very aware of the overall ideals of Girl Scouts, its history, and the international aspect of Girl Scouting. This troop was different. I realized that my goal assumed a lot that was not necessarily so.

I was not starting from scratch. I had not taken into account the fact that this troop had been going since September and I was coming in mid-

January. They had already established their own goals, or Judy had, and I did not agree with them. Judy had never been a Girl Scout, and her idea of a Girl Scout meeting was two hours of fun and games. Most of the girls did not know the Girl Scout Promise or the Law. I later learned from Lynn that Troop #3 had not participated in most of the Girl Scout events set up by the city's Girl Scout Council. Only a few of the girls had uniforms or Girl Scout handbooks. They had earned two badges in the fall, but they had not been ordered yet. As far as I could tell, they had done nothing but arts and crafts since Christmas—just for the fun of it.

After the first meeting, I talked with Judy to see what kinds of plans there were for the coming months; there were none. I made some suggestions to see how much she was going to let me do. She was enthusiastic about my knowledge of music: "Great, now they can learn some songs; the girls love that." But as far as my badge plans went, all she had to say was, "Just wait 'til I get to know you in a more quiet setting," which I interpreted to mean, "I don't trust you." I was a little surprised when she asked me to teach a song at the next meeting.

Given the situation I found at the first meeting, I had to set myself new goals. I was still stubbornly determined to teach the girls what Girl Scouting was all about. I began to brace myself for a difficult few months, trying to convince Judy that I was capable, responsible, and trustworthy. I was quite surprised at how quickly that happened. Dissension between the two of us was not an issue again until the campout.

I turned my attention to the girls. The dilemma that I ran into there was getting them to work together cooperatively. It seemed to me that they were always bickering, and there even seemed to be some who were set enemies. I was constantly looking for reasons for the arguments and ways to end them quickly without hurting anyone's feelings.

At one meeting three girls, Natalie, Mary, and Nicole, were not getting along. Natalie and Mary were both black—in fact, they were the only two black in the troop—and they were fast friends. Neither of them liked Nicole. I thought that perhaps Mary and Natalie had formed their little twosome because of their race. I did not know if there were any prejudices within this group, and this occurred to me as a possible reason for the discord between these girls.

Later, Mary and Nicole ended up next to each other in the circle but were visibly cringing away from each other. I ignored this, not wanting to make a big deal out of something that might solve itself. Then we had to pair up for a game, and Mary and Nicole were left.

Nicole said to me, "I don't have a partner."

"Neither does Mary," I said.

Natalie offered the information, "They hate each other."

I ignored them and started the game. I had been ignoring them because

I thought that they might be putting on an act for attention, and I did not want to give them that attention for fear that they would continue. But then two other girls separated so that Mary and Nicole would not have to play together. I began to think that if the other girls knew enough about the relationship between Nicole and Mary to want to keep them apart, there was something in it. If it was a long-standing dislike, could I hope to be able to do anything about it?

Later still, we had to divide into groups of three; Natalie and Nicole ended up in a group together.

Natalie said, "We don't get along."

Nicole said, "We won't get anything done because we don't talk to each other."

Lynn replied, "Well, you'll just have to try."

Natalie said, "My mother won't let me talk to her."

I asked, "Why not?" (I was suspicious, thinking that perhaps my race ideas went even further, stemming from parents' views.)

Natalie said, "We always end up fighting." (So it was just a mother as tired of listening to the bickering as I was.)

I said, "Part of Girl Scouts is learning to work with each other." (I talked about the ideals of Girl Scouting often, trying to show them that things would not work without their cooperation.)

Natalie said, "I just won't do anything."

Lynn replied, "You'll just have to work it out, won't you?"

As the weeks went by, similar situations arose, always between different girls, and I began to examine these situations as a whole rather than individually. I soon dismissed my race theory. There were plenty of interracial friendships and really no grounds for assuming there were prejudices. But my idea that they were being catty for attention seemed more realistic. Lynn and I had made it clear to Mary, Natalie, and Nicole what we thought and ignored them after that. The next week everything was fine with those three, but two others were arguing over something else.

Watching all this happen, I realized that there were no shy girls in the group. They all had opinions and expressed them loudly. With so many strongly opinionated girls, each with different interests and ideas, there were bound to be disagreements. I noticed, too, that there were considerably fewer arguments at the campout. I think that perhaps they were tired at the after-school meetings. They had spent the entire day in the classroom. Also, being outdoors rather than in a classroom, I think, made them feel less restricted.

I noticed that Judy sometimes played referee when an enormous disagreement stopped us from getting anything done. For example, one week they wanted to play a game called Four Square, but they could not agree on the rules and were screaming accusations and insults at each other. Judy shouted above all of them, "All right, everybody over here!" And she set up definite rules democratically: "How many people want the tea party rule? . . . one . . . two . . . three . . . okay, we play without it." It was effective, and I copied her later. I learned to put these arguments in perspective, and I paid attention to them only when they were seriously slowing everything down.

Another form of dissension formed between one of the girls, Erin, and me. I did not actually dislike her, but she was exceedingly annoying and her whining grated on my nerves. I am afraid I was sometimes short on patience in dealing with her. During the argument over the rules of the game, Erin screeched and whined. She was not very articulate and her tone of voice was rather unpleasant. The other girls tired of listening to her before she got a chance to make herself understood.

I figured that it was a matter of trying to get attention. She has twin sisters, six years old, and probably has to compete for parental attention at home. At first, I tried always to listen to her. I saw that if she knew one was listening, she would not whine. But I could not focus all my attention on her alone. As soon as I turned to another girl, her whining began again, and I began to ignore her for fear that in my irritation I would snap at her. Of course, this frustrated her even more. I had to juggle, giving her as much attention as possible, to avoid the whining, without being unfair to the other girls. I had to weight every situation, and I got better at it with practice.

At the campout, I noticed that the whining had diminished considerably. I attributed this to the different atmosphere, as I did with the arguing. Judy commented on it, too, and I found out that I was not the only one who had noticed this problem. Erin's teacher had mentioned it to her parents, and they were concerned about it and working on it with her. I would have liked to help, but I think that these people who came into contact with her daily had much more clout than I, who saw her only once a week. This was a problem that it was not my place to solve, nor would I have been very effective if I had tried.

As I mentioned before, conflict with Judy arose again at the campout. Judy was a little bit lazy; she just wanted to have fun. When she realized that I was willing to plan the meeting, she was happy to let me have the responsibility. I was always glad to have her around because she knew these girls well and knew how to handle the minor crises that came up. I learned from her how to do this, and later when Lynn and I ran a couple of meetings on our own, they went smoothly. Also, the girls liked Judy. She was fun, and was always ready to be silly and giggly with them.

Our first problem with the campout was driving. We were going to Judy's family's property on the lake near Bilden. Judy was rather irresponsible about the Girl Scout regulations. We, as leaders, are required to make sure that every girl in the car is wearing a seat belt, regardless of age or where they are seated. Also, there must be a signed permission slip for each girl in the car they are riding in. Judy wanted to pile all eleven girls into her station wagon. Lynn and I said no, we were not going to do that, and Judy could not see why. In the end we won, though; Judy, Lynn, and one mother were going to drive. Then one girl did not have a permission slip, and Judy told her to never mind, it did not matter. Lynn and I said, yes, it did matter. Judy was looking for ways to get around this regulation, and the girl ended up in tears because she thought it meant she could not go. Eventually, another mother who was there and who looked after this girl five afternoons a week signed a permission slip for her.

Judy's irresponsibility got to be even more of a problem when it came to issues of authority. For example, there was a rowboat on the shore, and the girls had asked Judy if they could go out in it. She said they could. She seldom said "no." I saw six girls climbing into a boat with no life jackets and no adult. I did not know that Judy had given permission.

"Wait! What are you guys doing?" I shouted.

Six voices answered, "Ms. Malloy said we could!"

I went to Judy while they were still struggling with the boat and said, "They're not supposed to go out without life jackets and an adult."

By this time Judy was fed up with what she called Lynn's and my regulations and said, "Well, then *you* go tell them they can't." So I was the "bad guy" who had spoiled their fun. I heard "But Ms. Malloy said we could!" too many times that weekend.

I am still not sure how I could have solved this problem with Judy. I think it was a conflict of personalities. I am systematic, organized, and perhaps overly cautious. Judy is irresponsible, spontaneous, and a lot of fun.

I realized very quickly that my original broad goal had to be broken down into smaller, more immediately attainable goals. I learned to settle dissension between the girls. For the most part I was able to hide my impatience with one girl in particular, and I did my best to give her the attention she needed. I was able to convince Judy that I was competent and our differences lay dormant through most of the semester. It was unfortunate that they came to a head at our last event, but this just showed me that a dilemma that seems to be solved can come up again.

A woman from the city's Girl Scout Council has asked me to help get a Cadette troop (seventh and eighth grade) started next fall. I will not have the same problems I had this spring. I will be starting from the beginning, myself. Therefore, I can make my own plans instead of trying to change something that I believe started off on the wrong foot. Because I will not be working with Judy, I will not find out if I could have solved that problem, but it will save me a great deal of frustration to be working on my own. I am hoping that the older girls will realize how important it is to work cooperatively. Also, girls who stay with Girl Scouts that long are usually serious about it. I really enjoyed working with this energetic group of girls, I grew fond of them, and I will miss them. All of the same, I am looking forward to next fall.

SAMPLE PROGRESS REPORT 5

By Juliet R. Johnson

Burton Middle School is a small urban school on the outskirts of Turner. It consists of a two-story building, playground, and parking lot. There is nothing on the outside of the building to set it apart as a school, but on one's entering the building, there is no mistaking its identity.

There are displays (mostly scientific) on many of the walls, the decor is innovative with multicolored walls, or walls with diagonal stripes, and even during class time there are always some students wandering in the hallway on their way to the library or whatever.

During class time there is a general "hum" of activity, but at recess and lunchtime the noise level rises considerably. The halls are kept quite tidy and free from litter—the rules about littering seem to be well enforced or well observed (or both).

Although discipline appears to be less needed as in, say an urban school in a large city, there are still set rules and regulations. The vice principal deals with any major infractions of these rules, with the most common punishment being time spent in the "Time Out Room." The older students help with disciplinary matters. Hall and lunchroom monitors make sure that the halls are kept tidy, and a general sense of order is maintained.

The whole atmosphere of the school is very relaxed and comfortable. Joking between the staff and students is a common form of exchange, but at the same time there is also a mutual respect present which I think is one of the prime reasons for the good student–teacher relationships that exist. Another factor which probably accounts for the open atmosphere is that the school is quite small and the impression that I obtained was that everyone knows just about everyone else, students and staff alike.

The relaxed atmosphere extends into the classroom, although I had only one opportunity to actually sit in on a class. My contact with teachers was minimal, in fact my "contact" at the school was the guidance counselor. Derek and Wally (the two students that I tutored) had approached her to ask for help in their studies and thus it was through her that I heard about the opportunity. We met in the library on Tuesdays and Thursdays for 45 minutes each session. Neither the situation nor the time was ideal, but there was nothing that could be done about it. The time was really too short for us to get very much accomplished and I was very conscious of the time limit that we had. The library was not the best of places for serious learning to take place. There were too many distractions—students talking in the library (the rules there were not observed at all, if there were any) and friends of Derek and Wally were continually coming up to us and interrupting the session. Although I did mention this a few times to Tess (the guidance counselor) it seemed like there was really no other place available. And so we weathered out the semester in the library as best as we could.

I had several goals for my field experience. Some were well defined in my mind—I knew exactly what I wanted to achieve—and some were a bit vague—I had an idea of what I wanted to happen but I wasn't too sure of how to achieve that. One of my major goals was to create an atmosphere in our sessions so that the boys would be really interested in learning. I wanted to try to help them enjoy the subject so that learning about it would not be a task for them. This goal has not been changed for me, although I think it has been slightly modified. I realize now that such a situation is difficult to "create." There is a certain amount of preparation that can be done to set this up, but a part of it also has to occur naturally. In fact, some of the best learning experiences occurred unexpectedly with no preparation beforehand.

At the beginning of my field experience I knew what kind of a relationship I wanted with the students. I would have a certain amount of control over the sessions—they wouldn't be allowed to get out of hand—but at the same time I wanted to be a good friend to them. I think I sort of wanted to have the respect that they showed toward a teacher and at the same time be on familiar enough terms with them so that they would feel free to talk to me about anything. Now I realize that such a goal was a bit unrealistic. I found myself not wanting to say anything to their friends when they interrupted us for fear of "falling out of favor" with them. So this goal was also modified by my field experience. I still maintain the belief that a student and teacher should be on good terms, but not to the extent that the student begins to lose respect for the teacher.

Another of my goals was that I would give each student whatever individual attention he required to grasp the basic concepts of a topic. However, when I started my field experience I had no idea how difficult this would be even with two students at varying learning levels. But although it was not easy to practice, my belief in this goal has in fact been strengthened from my field experience. Even though this brought up the question of "breadth versus depth" as well as putting a strain on the time limit, I realize even more now how important it is to spend the extra time with slower learners.

I guess that one of my main goals was not a conscious one but instead an underlying one in that I wanted the boys to understand what I was trying to teach them. But I think that this is a rather unspoken goal of most teachers, although during the first teaching experiences it seems terribly important, since our teaching ability is based on how well our students have learned the material. Another somewhat general goal that I had was that I wanted to be fully prepared for every session. I still have both of these goals and I expect that I will as long as I am teaching.

My field experience taught me many things about teaching. Although I was not actually teaching in a classroom with a cooperating teacher, problems and situations arose which were similar to those that would be encountered in a classroom. In a way I'm glad that my teaching experience was on a small scale: it gently opened my eyes to some real dilemmas that arise in teaching.

One thing that I learned somewhat too late in my experience was that being a friend to your students is good, but not to the extent that you're afraid to exercise some authority over them. And I now realize that it is very important to have some control over a class, no matter how small it is. There were times when, because of a lack of authority on my part, I felt very inadequate and I think at such times I lost a bit of respect in the stuents' eyes (although at the time that didn't occur to me).

What really brought this home to me was something that occurred in our last session. I hadn't said anything to the boys about their friends' interrupting, since I was sure that they sensed how I felt. But on my last day with them, we were in the middle of our lesson when two girls walked up to Derek and started talking to him. What really annoyed me was that Derek conversed with them for a while and then asked them if they wanted to join us. Of course they did, which did not improve the boy's concentration on the lesson. I didn't say anything to them, especially since it was my last day, but nevertheless I was quite angry—both at Derek for interrupting our lesson and seeming to place little importance on what we were doing and at myself for not having said anything about it before. I was always too afraid that if I did say anything I would lose their trust and friendship—as it was I lost some of my self-respect, and somehow I think that the boys would have respected me more had I said something.

Similar situations could arise in a classroom. However since there are more students in a classroom, the student–teacher relationship would probably not be as close, and it would be more difficult for the teacher to be a "friend." Also, different students would require different degrees of discipline and so the teacher would have to "tailor" his or her output to the needs of the student.

One particularly good learning experience that I had proved to me that extra time spent explaining something, even if it detracts from moving ahead to cover more material, is usually well worth it. I strongly believe that it is desirable to help a student to understand a concept that he or she is finding difficult. Although this may result in some of the material not being covered fully, I think that understanding especially basic concepts of a topic helps a student to get a much better overall understanding of the subject.

One particular experience that I had occurred when Derek was having problems balancing scientific equations. I didn't expect that he'd have problems—Wally didn't and I thought it was pretty simple. But for some reason, Derek just couldn't seem to understand the logic behind it. I spent most of two sessions trying to explain it to him and he was still confused. I was really worried that I wouldn't be able to get through to him on this topic but I didn't know what to do. Finally in the third session I just used several different ideas and models, and for some reason something suddenly clicked for him and he finally understood what was going on. We were both so relieved and happy—Derek because he'd grasped something that beforehand had made no sense to him, and me because I had managed to help him to understand and hadn't failed him or myself.

The problem of helping slow learners is applicable especially to larger classes. I was able to keep Wally fairly busy while trying to help Derek, but this would probably be almost impossible to do with a large class. I also think that is a problem that is encountered very often in many teaching situations, and each teacher just has to decide on his/her method of dealing with it.

One thing that I learned by trial and error is that it is always best to admit that you're not sure of a particular topic instead of trying to "fudge" your way through. If you do try to pretend that you know what you're talking about, it only results in everyone—including yourself—being totally confused. Some respect is lost—your own as well as the students' toward you.

I did this on one occasion: I was explaining something to the boys when a question came up that I was unsure of. I tried to stumble through the explanation, not wanting to admit that I was unsure of myself, and eventually all three of us were quite confused. Finally I asked for time out, reread the explanation in the text, and started over once I understood what was going on. I felt much better about it.

I feel that this is applicable to all situations and not just teaching. No one knows everything there is to know about a subject and therefore everyone should be able to admit when he or she doesn't know something. Of course I now realize that this is easier said than done.

It's always good to just relax and talk about something different, and I didn't realize how applicable this was to teaching until I began my field experience. Particularly if the students were really working and not just wasting time, it is nice to "break" in a lesson every once in a while. Also, if the students are in a particularly skittish mood (which is understandable just before a vacation) chances are that they won't do very much work anyway and the teacher will only acquire a set of very frayed nerves.

One incident that helped me see this occurred just after the boys had returned to school after a long weekend. They were particularly talkative and couldn't seem to settle down to work. I began to get a bit exasperated until suddenly I realized that the best thing to do would be to let them talk and get it out of their system, and then return to the lesson. It worked quite nicely since it gave me an opportunity to get to know the boys a little better and for them to tell me something about themselves.

This would probably be less applicable to a more structured situation, such as a classroom. After all, if a break were called everytime someone was in a talkative mood, there would be no work done. But in small groups I think that it works quite well.

Like most other people, I did not achieve all of the goals which I set for myself. This is largely due to the fact that this was my first "teaching" experience and so I wasn't quite sure what to expect. One area in which I failed was that of control. Although I didn't want to dominate the sessions, I did want to have a certain amount of authority. But I didn't because I became too much of a "friend." I guess my goal of having just enough authority and being a friend was more difficult to achieve than I expected. But I also think that a part of this was due to my lack of confidence in myself as a teacher.

At the beginning of my field experience, I was determined to be fully prepared for every session and I wasn't. There were times when I prepared the wrong chapter, had been sick, or had a lot of other work to do and was therefore unable to spend as much time preparing for the session as I wanted to. But I guess I just didn't take into account such factors as health, other work, and a breakdown in communications between myself and the boys as far as knowing what chapter to prepare from week to week.

One goal which I didn't even realize until quite late in my field experience was that I wanted to prepare the boys to continue working on their own after I left. I just didn't realize how much they depended on me to help them with extra work until nearly the end of the semester when I started to realize what my leaving would mean to them. I also didn't anticipate the sense of responsibility that I would feel towards them or the feeling that I was deserting them when I left. I'd heard excerpts from logs of previous students who'd felt really guilty about leaving their students at the end of the semester, but it never occurred to me that it would happen in my situation. So although I feel that my field experience was very valuable in that I learned a lot from it, and although I believe that I did something that was worthwhile, there is one part of it that I disliked very much, and that was having to end it.

SAMPLE PROGRESS REPORT 6

By Paul Reed

Context

Memorial High School is a large, multi-building school serving almost all of Lakeside's high school students. Administratively, there is poor control in the fashion of a top-down management approach. Many of the teachers despise this ruling but do nothing about it. This affects the teachers' relationships with their students in a negative way and causes a strain on the whole system of education, making the atmosphere in some classrooms heated and not conducive to studying.

I taught tenth-grade biology, with Sandra Petre, to track 2 and track 3 students. Many of them are in the class only because it is required for graduation. In short, about 95 percent of the kids are there just wasting time until they are old enough to quit. The students come from all walks of life. In my classes alone, I have kids who grew up in street gangs from New York City, kids from California, one from the South, and a few from overseas. Many are from economically disadvantaged homes or no home at all. Some have lost one or both of their parents to death or divorce. A few of the girls are pregnant, and a few of the guys are fathers. Some have attempted suicide; one succeeded.

Sandra tries to help the kids accept reality by dealing with them on a person-to-person basis, not the usual student-to-teacher basis. Her informal style of teaching and genuine concern for the kids have helped many of them cope with school and life. She allows each student the freedom to develop to his or her maximum and holds each one responsible for himself or herself. Her respect for the students is reflected by their respect for her and their increase in ability to do school work after being in her class, as reflected by improved grades in other courses, as well as biology.

Goals

I met my first day of field experience with much apprehension and excitement. I wasn't quite sure what was expected of me nor what I was to expect from it. I had spent the previous summer trying to decide if veterinary medicine was a good career choice or not. In the back of my mind I had always thought of being a teacher but wasn't sure if it was the right thing for me. Trying to choose one of the alternatives was not easy.

My major goals centered around these mixed and unsure feelings I had about career choices. Primarily, my goals were to find out what teaching looked like from behind the desk, whether I really wanted to teach, and whether I really could teach so people would understand me. In addition to that, I had smaller secondary goals such as defining a perspective and style of teaching unique to me and developing a rapport with the students so they would trust me. An ideal goal of mine was to have all my students understand me and listen to all the (good?) advice I had to pass along to them about education, school, and life in general.

Learning

On teaching . . .

The single most important idea I learned during this field experience is that teaching is the right choice for me. I was really undecided about this decision, and I wasn't getting much favorable input from parents. However, a few episodes helped reassure me that education was a correct choice for me.

A big step in this direction was all the smiles and thanks I received from my students. One time was when Andy was having trouble working out Punnet Squares in genetics. I went over to help him during class and spent that time teaching Punnet Squares as if they were simple multiplication tables. When he left class, he was so proud of himself that he smiled and told Sandra that they were easy. Another time was when I helped Tom from Period 5. He was having trouble understanding a lab, so I went over to explain it to him. After our discussion, I left him and helped someone else. At the end of the period, Tom came up to me, smiled, said "Thanks!" and left. But I think the time that hit home the most was when Tom from Period 2 attemped suicide. As the kids were sending around a get well card, one of them brought it over to me and asked me to sign it. To be accepted by the kids as one of them is one of the biggest thrills I could imagine for a beginning teacher.

Aside from these student episodes, some personal milestones were made. I found that I could really teach when I had to give a lecture on excretion and wasn't prepared for it. I had taught the students before, but I had always been prepared by reading the text, taking notes, reading my personal texts, and preparing a lecture outline. Sandra surprised me by telling me to teach without giving me notice. Period 3 came, and it was "sink or swim." Fortunately, I swam. From this small incident, I learned that I could teach, and I did not have to rely on the text. It also showed me that I cared enough about teaching to do it properly.

I know these little things don't happen frequently, but once in a while is good enough for me. All I need is something to remind me of how lucky I am and how much some kids do appreciate my teaching skills.

On discipline . . .

Another idea that confronted me was discipline. Prior to my teaching experience, I didn't think much about this aspect of education. Our school didn't have a severe discipline problem (at least not in my classes), so I thought it was the exception rather than the rule. I had another thing coming. Many of the kids grew up in Harlem or other ghetto districts and have been in street gangs or other rough groups. The hardest thing for me was to try to discipline one of the guys. If you ask them nicely, they respond with a cordial "No!" or "Why?" I knew that raising my voice wouldn't work, so I tried several other tactics. The three I found most productive were: trying to talk calmly with them, using the silent treatment, and relying on "threats." For going into education with no discipline tactics and coming out with three fairly good ones, I feel as if I learned a great deal.

On pacing and style . . .

Another skill/idea that was presented and resolved dealt with the pace of the lecture. The ideal would be to have a pace so that all the students could learn at the same time without any getting bored and feeling that they were too far behind to bother. This ideal is probably never attained, except maybe in a one-to-one tutorial. I guess I have been trained throughout my college career to go fast so you can cover as much material as possible. That way, nobody has the time to get bored. Along with this goes the style of teaching whereby nothing gets put onto the blackboard unless it is very important. I look on this as my beginning style and taught my first class this way. From the looks that some of the kids were giving me, I sensed that something was wrong, so I slowed down my delivery rate, and the kids began to look happier.

For the next period, I decided to teach by listing important terms on the blackboard. This was easier for me to follow because it was simple to see how one concept flowed into another. I didn't need to look at my notes as much, which helped my credibility with the kids, and I felt more comfortable with this style of teaching. Also, I slowed my rate of delivery and the kids seemed to follow me more easily.

Of all my ideas, the one on style and pace changed the most. I certainly learned from my field experience in this case. I entered the position with one style in mind and I had made a drastic, 180 degree turnaround to a style that the students and I were very comfortable with.

Generalizability

It is hard to say how general my learning was. I have to admit that I was dealing with a very special and specific group of kids, but the things I learned in my classes this semester could have been learned by any person in almost any situation. Also, everything I learned is applicable to other teaching situations in one degree or another. A few episodes that I was confronted with probably don't happen too often, but I am glad I was exposed to them with a wonderful cooperating teacher to back me up!

Goal Attainment

As I reflect over the past semester, I realize that my goals were quite straightforward on their orientation. I feel as if I obtained my goals and made a few major decisions along the way. Along with these decisions, I also developed my own style and delivery, perspective, and relationship with my kids.

Now that I've been behind the desk looking out into the classroom, I know that teaching is the option for me. I certainly was tested by my kids, Sandra, and myself. The hardest test to pass was my own, but I feel now that I can teach and do it to the best of my ability. This field experience is one of the most beneficial of all of my happenings at college.

Suggested Reading

Axline, V. *Dibs: In Search of Self*. Boston: Houghton Mifflin, 1964.
    A gripping case study of the use of client-centered play therapy in the treatment of one psychologically disturbed young boy.

Berlak, A., and H. Berlak. *Dilemmas of Schooling*. London: Methuen, 1981.
    This book begins with a detailed description of British primary school situations. The authors use this descriptive data to construct a framework for examining schooling, a set of sixteen "dilemmas" that all teachers face daily.

Cooper, J. *Classroom Teaching Skills,* 2nd ed. Lexington, Mass.: D. C. Heath, 1982.
    Contains many useful exercises for developing teaching skills.

Duck, L. *Teaching with Charisma*. Boston: Allyn and Bacon, 1981.
    An engaging approach to the philosophy of teaching.

Duke, D., and A. Meckel. *Teachers' Guide to Classroom Management*. New York: Random House, 1984.
    A basic text on maintaining control in the classroom.

Grant, C., ed. *Preparing for Reflective Teaching*. Boston: Allyn and Bacon, 1984.
    A book of thought-provoking readings on teaching. The lead article by Grant and Zeichner is a must.

Posner, G. *Course Design,* 3rd ed. New York: Longman, 1986.
    A basic how-to-do-it approach to curriculum development.

Ryan, E., *et al. Biting the Apple*. New York: Longman, 1980.
    Twelve first-year teachers describe the positive and negative experiences during their induction into the teaching profession. The book covers a wide range of issues.

Schwebel, A., *et al. The Student Teacher Handbook*. New York: Barnes and Noble, 1979.

One of the few basic guides to student teaching. Covers most of the problems that arise.

Sizer, Theodore R. *Horace's Compromise: The Dilemma of the American High School.* Boston: Houghton Mifflin, 1985.

One of the most compelling analyses of secondary education in the United States. Of all the many current school reform proposals, Sizer's report is the most comprehensive and disturbing. The readers will have to judge the merits of his recommendations.

Weathersby, R., P. Allen, and A. Blackmer. *New Roles for Educators.* Cambridge, Mass.: Harvard Graduate School Placement Office, 1970.

A comprehensive resource for persons prepared in education but desiring unconventional careers (i.e., not school teaching). The book covers industry, government, schools, nonprofit associations, and community organizations and offers individual profiles of individuals who have found these nonteaching jobs.

Wigginton, E. *Sometimes a Shining Moment.* New York: Doubleday Books, 1987.

On the one hand, this book represents one educator's perspective on teaching. On the other hand, it is the story behind the Foxfire books. An account of a truly courageous and gifted teacher's development of an experiential education program that has inspired several hundred Foxfire-type programs across the United States.

Index

DATE DUE

GAYLORD			PRINTED IN U.S.A.